The Secret Language of Birthdays April Profiles

Birthdays Profiles

Daniel Sanjurjo

Published by Daniel Sanjurjo, 2024.

Table of Contents

Introduction

Unveiling the Cosmic Secrets of April Births

Welcome, dear readers, to a cosmic journey through the enchanting realms of those born in the month of April. As your guide, I bring you insider insights into the intricate tapestry of personalities, destinies, and peculiar quirks that distinguish Aries and Taurus individuals born during this magical month.

Consider me your celestial confidant, armed with exclusive knowledge about the spirited Aries souls igniting the early days of April and the grounded Taurus gems adorning the latter part. What unfolds in these pages is more than a mere exploration; it's a cosmic revelation, a peek behind the celestial curtain.

As we navigate the vibrant energy of Aries—bold, impulsive, and fueled by the fire of passion—and then seamlessly transition into the steadfast realm of Taurus—practical, determined, and grounded in the earth's embrace—you'll find yourself immersed in the intricate dance of cosmic forces.

So, buckle up, intrepid readers! Get ready to unravel the mysteries, embrace the eccentricities, and celebrate the unique charm that April-born individuals bring to the world. This book is not just about zodiac signs; it's a journey into the very essence of April souls, where every page holds a nugget of wisdom, a burst of laughter, and a cosmic secret waiting to be unveiled.

Are you ready to explore the cosmic wonders of April births? Turn the page, and let the celestial adventure begin!

The book "The Secret Language of Birthdays April Profiles: Unlocking Your Unique Traits" is all about understanding why birthdays are so special and how they play a role in shaping who we are. Imagine your birthday as a key that unlocks the door to your unique personality traits. This book takes you on a journey to explore the significance of birthdays and how they have the power to mold and influence your character.

Birthdays are more than just cake and presents; they carry a hidden magic that affects our lives in surprising ways. By delving into the secrets of astrology, numerology, and other fascinating elements, this book aims to unravel the mysteries behind your birthdate. We'll explore how the alignment of the stars, the energy of numbers, and the elements associated with your birthday contribute to the wonderful tapestry of your personality.

Whether you're curious about why certain zodiac signs share common traits or interested in how your birthdate can influence your relationships, "The Secret Language of Birthdays April Profiles" has got you covered. It's a journey of self-discovery, helping you recognize and appreciate the unique qualities that make you who you are.

So, if you've ever wondered why people born on the same day can be so different, join us on this adventure. Let's celebrate the significance of birthdays and uncover the extraordinary aspects that make each of us beautifully distinct. Get ready to embrace the magic of your own birthday profile!

Explanation of the concept of birthday profiles

So, what exactly are birthday profiles? Picture them as personalized snapshots of your personality based on the magical combination of your birthdate and the cosmic forces at play. In 'The Secret Language of Birthdays April Profiles,' we dive into the concept of birthday profiles to reveal the unique traits and influences that shape who you are.

Your birthday profile is like a cosmic fingerprint, capturing the essence of your individuality. It's a blend of insights from astrology, numerology, and the elements associated with your birthdate. By exploring these aspects, we can uncover the hidden layers of your personality and understand why you might share certain characteristics with others born on the same day.

Think of your birthday profile as a cosmic roadmap guiding you through the quirks and qualities that set you apart. From zodiac signs to numerology vibes and astrological elements, each piece contributes to the colorful mosaic of your being. It's a fascinating journey of self-discovery, allowing you to embrace the uniqueness that makes you, well, you.

So, get ready to explore your very own birthday profile in 'The Secret Language of Birthdays April Profiles.' It's like unwrapping a special gift from the universe, revealing the extraordinary details that make your personality shine!

Explore the cultural and historical significance of celebrating birthdays.

Let's take a trip through time and traditions to uncover the cultural and historical significance of celebrating birthdays. In 'The Secret Language of Birthdays April Profiles,' we venture into the rich tapestry of customs and beliefs that have shaped the way we commemorate the day we entered this world.

Throughout history, various cultures have attached profound meaning to birthdays. In ancient civilizations, birthdays were often linked to religious or spiritual beliefs, signifying a person's connection to divine forces. As societies evolved, so did the ways in which birthdays were celebrated, from grand feasts to simple gatherings with loved ones.

The concept of birthday cakes and candles has its roots in Ancient Greece, where people offered round-shaped cakes adorned with candles to honor the moon goddess Artemis. Fast-forward to today, and blowing out candles on a cake has become a cherished birthday ritual, symbolizing the passing of another year and making a wish for the future.

In many cultures, reaching specific ages holds special significance. In some East Asian cultures, a baby's first birthday, known as the Doljanchi, is a grand celebration symbolizing good fortune and longevity. In the Jewish tradition, a Bar or Bat Mitzvah marks a coming-of-age milestone.

As we celebrate birthdays today with parties, gifts, and joyous gatherings, it's worth acknowledging the historical threads that connect us to ancient practices. 'The Secret Language of Birthdays April Profiles' unfolds these cultural layers, allowing you to appreciate the diverse and meaningful ways people have marked the passage of time and the celebration of life across different eras and regions. So, join us in exploring the fascinating cultural and historical tapestry woven into the fabric of birthday celebrations!

Overview of the zodiac signs and their impact on personality

Let's dive into the captivating world of the zodiac signs and unravel how they influence our personalities in 'The Secret Language of Birthdays April Profiles.' Imagine the zodiac as a celestial personality chart, with each sign having its unique traits and characteristics that leave an indelible mark on those born under its influence.

Aries (March 21 - April 19): Picture the energetic and adventurous Aries, symbolized by the ram. Known for their boldness and enthusiasm, Aries individuals often lead with passion and courage.

Taurus (April 20 - May 20): Enter the stable and grounded realm of Taurus, represented by the bull. Taurus folks are known for their practicality, determination, and appreciation for life's comforts.

Gemini (May 21 - June 20): Meet the social butterflies of the zodiac, the Gemini twins. With a dual nature, Geminis are versatile, communicative, and love to explore various aspects of life.

Cancer (June 21 - July 22): Step into the nurturing embrace of Cancer, symbolized by the crab. Cancers are known for their emotional depth, intuition, and strong connections to home and family.

Leo (July 23 - August 22): Embrace the fiery energy of Leo, the lion. Leos are charismatic, confident, and often take center stage with their bold and vibrant personalities.

Virgo (August 23 - September 22): Enter the analytical and detail-oriented world of Virgo. Symbolized by the maiden, Virgos are known for their practicality, precision, and strong sense of duty.

Libra (September 23 - October 22): Explore the balanced and harmonious realm of Libra, symbolized by the scales. Libras value fairness, beauty, and strive for peaceful relationships.

Scorpio (October 23 - November 21): Plunge into the intense and transformative energy of Scorpio, represented by the scorpion. Scorpios are known for their depth, passion, and mystery.

Sagittarius (November 22 - December 21): Join the adventurous and optimistic Sagittarius, symbolized by the archer. Sanitarians love exploration, freedom, and have a philosophical outlook on life.

Capricorn (December 22 - January 19): Ascend to the disciplined and ambitious world of Capricorn, symbolized by the goat. Capricorns are known for their determination, responsibility, and strong work ethic.

Aquarius (January 20 - February 18): Immerse yourself in the innovative and humanitarian spirit of Aquarius, represented by the water bearer. Aquarians are known for their originality, independence, and love for social causes.

Pisces (February 19 - March 20): Dive into the dreamy and empathetic world of Pisces, symbolized by the fish. Pisceans are known for their creativity, compassion, and intuitive nature.

In 'The Secret Language of Birthdays April Profiles,' we explore how the position of the sun at your birth within this zodiacal tapestry contributes to your unique personality traits. It's like discovering the cosmic fingerprints that shape who you are!

Descriptions of each zodiac sign's traits and tendencies.

Certainly! Let's delve into the distinct traits and tendencies of each zodiac sign in 'The Secret Language of Birthdays April Profiles':

1. Aries (March 21 - April 19):

   • Traits: Energetic, adventurous, and bold.

   • Tendencies: Aries individuals are natural leaders, known for their courage, enthusiasm, and a go-getter attitude.

2. Taurus (April 20 - May 20):

   • Traits: Stable, grounded, and practical.

   • Tendencies: Taurus individuals are reliable and enjoy the comforts of life. They are determined, patient, and often have a strong connection to nature.

3. Gemini (May 21 - June 20):

   • Traits: Social, adaptable, and communicative.

   • Tendencies: Geminis are versatile and enjoy engaging with others. They have a curious nature, love learning, and may pursue various interests simultaneously.

4. Cancer (June 21 - July 22):

- Traits: Nurturing, intuitive, and emotional.

- Tendencies: Cancers are deeply connected to their emotions and family. They are protective, empathetic, and value a sense of security in their relationships.

5. Leo (July 23 - August 22):

- Traits: Charismatic, confident, and vibrant.

- Tendencies: Leos love the spotlight, exuding warmth and energy. They are natural leaders, generous, and enjoy creative pursuits.

6. Virgo (August 23 - September 22):

- Traits: Analytical, detail-oriented, and practical.

- Tendencies: Virgos are meticulous and have a keen eye for detail. They value organization, reliability, and often excel in analytical tasks.

7. Libra (September 23 - October 22):

- Traits: Balanced, diplomatic, and sociable.

- Tendencies: Libras seek harmony and balance in relationships. They are cooperative, appreciate beauty, and have a strong sense of justice.

8. Scorpio (October 23 - November 21):

- Traits: Intense, passionate, and mysterious.

- Tendencies: Scorpios are deep thinkers, often with a magnetic and transformative presence. They value authenticity, loyalty, and are drawn to the profound aspects of life.

9. Sagittarius (November 22 - December 21):

- Traits: Adventurous, optimistic, and philosophical.

- Tendencies: Sagittarians have a love for exploration, freedom, and a philosophical outlook. They are open-minded, enthusiastic, and enjoy learning from diverse experiences.

10. Capricorn (December 22 - January 19):

- Traits: Disciplined, ambitious, and responsible.

- Tendencies: Capricorns are hardworking and value structure. They are determined to achieve their goals, often displaying resilience and a strong sense of responsibility.

11. Aquarius (January 20 - February 18):

- Traits: Innovative, independent, and humanitarian.

- Tendencies: Aquarians are forward-thinking, embracing originality and independence. They are often drawn to social causes, with a vision for positive change.

12. Pisces (February 19 - March 20):

- Traits: Creative, compassionate, and intuitive.

• Tendencies: Pisceans are imaginative and empathetic, often drawn to artistic pursuits. They are compassionate, sensitive, and attuned to the emotions of others.

Each zodiac sign contributes its unique flavor to the cosmic cocktail of personalities. In 'The Secret Language of Birthdays April Profiles,' we explore how these traits intertwine with your birth date to create a one-of-a-kind recipe for your individuality!

How the position of the sun at your birth influences your characteristics.

Let's unravel the magic of how the position of the sun at your birth influences your characteristics in 'The Secret Language of Birthdays April Profiles.' Think of the sun as a cosmic spotlight, casting its warm glow on the unique traits that define you.

1. **Sun Sign Influence:**

   • Your sun sign represents the zodiac sign the sun was in at the time of your birth.

   • It plays a significant role in shaping your core personality and expressing your individuality.

2. **Energy and Vitality:**

   • The sun symbolizes energy and vitality, reflecting the essence of who you are at your core.

   • Its position at your birth is like a celestial stamp, marking the fundamental qualities that make you shine.

3. **Dominant Traits:**

- The characteristics associated with your sun sign become dominant features of your personality.

- For example, if you're a Leo, the sun's influence may infuse you with confidence, charisma, and a vibrant spirit.

4. Creative Expression:

- The sun's position influences how you express yourself creatively and how you approach various aspects of life.

- It shapes your preferences, strengths, and areas where you may naturally excel.

5. Personal Identity:

- Your sun sign contributes to your sense of self and personal identity.

- It reflects the qualities you are likely to resonate with and how you navigate the world around you.

6. Life Purpose and Goals:

- The sun's position can offer insights into your life purpose and the goals you may find fulfilling.

- It guides you toward areas of life where you can make a meaningful impact.

7. Interactions with Others:

- The sun sign also influences your interactions with others, shaping your approach to relationships and collaborations.

• It can provide clues about your strengths in communication, empathy, or leadership.

8. Personal Growth:

• Understanding the influence of the sun at your birth allows for personal growth and self-awareness.

• It's a tool for recognizing your strengths, embracing challenges, and evolving into the best version of yourself.

In 'The Secret Language of Birthdays April Profiles,' we explore how the sun's position adds its unique touch to your birthday profile, creating a personalized cosmic narrative. So, get ready to bask in the celestial glow of your sun sign and uncover the radiant qualities that make you distinctly you!

Introduction to numerology and its role in understanding personality.

Let's open the door to the intriguing world of numerology in 'The Secret Language of Birthdays April Profiles' and explore how numbers play a captivating role in understanding and shaping our personalities. Numerology is like a cosmic code that unveils the unique vibrations associated with your birth date, offering insights into the essence of who you are.

1. **Numerology Basics:**

   • Numerology involves assigning significance to numbers and understanding their energetic influences.

   • Each number carries a distinct vibration, contributing to the cosmic symphony that shapes your personality.

2. **Birthdate Numbers:**

   • In numerology, your birth date holds a special key to unlocking your unique traits.

   • By breaking down the digits of your birth date, we can unveil the specific vibrations associated with each component.

3. Life Path Number:

• The life path number is a central aspect of numerology, derived from your birth date.

• It represents the path you are destined to follow in life, offering insights into your purpose and journey.

4. Expression Number:

• The expression number, also known as the destiny number, reveals how you express yourself to the world.

• It reflects your strengths, talents, and the qualities you naturally embody.

5. Personality Traits:

• Numerology provides a framework for understanding your personality traits based on the energetic qualities associated with numbers.

• Each number corresponds to specific characteristics that add layers to your overall profile.

6. Compatibility Insights:

• Numerology extends its influence to relationships, offering insights into compatibility between individuals.

• By comparing life path numbers, we can explore the dynamics and challenges within different connections.

7. Personal Growth and Challenges:

• Numerology is not just about strengths; it also sheds light on areas for personal growth and challenges.

• It serves as a guide for self-improvement and understanding how to navigate life's journey.

8. Holistic Understanding:

• Combining numerology with other elements like astrology and the zodiac enhances the depth of our understanding.

• It creates a holistic and personalized approach to unraveling the intricate layers of your personality.

In 'The Secret Language of Birthdays April Profiles,' we embark on a numerical exploration to decode the vibrations connected to your birth date. Get ready to embrace the enchanting world of numerology and uncover the numeric patterns that contribute to the masterpiece of your personality!

Explanation of how birthdate numbers carry unique vibrations.

Let's unravel the mystical concept of how birthdate numbers carry unique vibrations in 'The Secret Language of Birthdays April Profiles.' It's like understanding the cosmic language encoded within the digits of the day you came into this world.

1. **Numerical Blueprint:**

  • Each digit in your birthdate, from the day to the month and year, carries a distinct energetic vibration.

  • This creates a numerical blueprint that influences your personality, traits, and life's journey.

2. **Day Number Significance:**

  • The day you were born holds its own vibration, representing your external personality and how you interact with the world.

  • For example, if you were born on the 5th, the energy associated with the number 5 adds its unique flavor to your character.

3. **Month Number Influence:**

• The month of your birth contributes another layer of vibrations.

• Each month is associated with a specific numeric energy, further shaping aspects of your personality and preferences.

4. Year Number Essence:

• The year of your birth holds a broader influence, shaping your overall life path and destiny.

• It encapsulates the lessons, challenges, and opportunities you are likely to encounter throughout your journey.

5. Life Path Number Calculation:

• One of the key numerical insights in numerology is the calculation of the life path number.

• By reducing the digits of your birthdate to a single-digit or master number, we unveil the core essence of your life's purpose and direction.

6. Energetic Combinations:

• The combination of these birthdate numbers creates a unique symphony of energies that resonates with your individuality.

• It's like a cosmic melody, where each note contributes to the overall composition of your personality.

7. Patterns and Cycles:

• Numerology recognizes patterns and cycles in your life based on these birthdate vibrations.

• These cycles offer insights into periods of growth, challenges, and transformation.

8. **Personalized Insights:**

• The beauty of birthdate numbers lies in their personalization — no two individuals have the same numeric composition.

• It's a personalized cosmic code that offers insights into your strengths, challenges, and the unique path you are meant to walk.

In 'The Secret Language of Birthdays April Profiles,' we decode these numerical vibrations to create a personalized narrative that reflects the essence of your being. Get ready to explore the enchanting world where numbers come to life and carry the unique energy of your birthdate!

Explore the significance of specific numbers in shaping individual traits.

Let's uncover the captivating significance of specific numbers in shaping individual traits in 'The Secret Language of Birthdays April Profiles.' Each number carries its own unique energy, influencing different aspects of your personality and life journey.

1. **Number 1: The Leader:**

   • Associated Traits: Independence, leadership, originality.

   • Significance: The number 1 brings a pioneering spirit, fostering traits of self-confidence, innovation, and a natural inclination to take the lead.

2. **Number 2: The Harmonizer:**

   • Associated Traits: Cooperation, diplomacy, sensitivity.

   • Significance: Number 2 is all about balance and collaboration, fostering traits of empathy, teamwork, and a knack for creating harmony in relationships.

3. **Number 3: The Creative Communicator:**

   • Associated Traits: Creativity, expression, optimism.

• Significance: Number 3 carries a vibrant energy, influencing traits like creativity, communication skills, and an optimistic outlook on life.

4. **Number 4: The Practical Builder:**

• Associated Traits: Practicality, stability, hard work.

• Significance: Number 4 represents a solid foundation, shaping traits such as diligence, practical thinking, and a strong work ethic.

5. **Number 5: The Adventurer:**

• Associated Traits: Freedom, versatility, curiosity.

• Significance: Number 5 brings a sense of adventure, influencing traits of versatility, a love for exploration, and a desire for freedom.

6. **Number 6: The Nurturer:**

• Associated Traits: Responsibility, compassion, family-oriented.

• Significance: Number 6 embodies a nurturing energy, shaping traits like responsibility, compassion, and a strong connection to family.

7. **Number 7: The Seeker of Knowledge:**

• Associated Traits: Introspection, wisdom, spiritual insight.

• Significance: Number 7 is linked to a quest for understanding, fostering traits of introspection, wisdom, and a deep connection to spiritual insights.

8. **Number 8: The Achiever:**

• Associated Traits: Ambition, success, self-discipline.

• Significance: Number 8 carries an energy of achievement, shaping traits like ambition, a strong sense of self-discipline, and a drive for success.

9. **Number 9: The Humanitarian:**

• Associated Traits: Compassion, altruism, idealism.

• Significance: Number 9 is linked to humanitarian pursuits, influencing traits of compassion, altruism, and a desire to contribute to the greater good.

10. **Master Number 11: The Intuitive Illuminator:**

• Associated Traits: Intuition, spiritual insight, enlightenment.

• Significance: Master Number 11 is a spiritually charged number, shaping traits of heightened intuition, deep insight, and a quest for enlightenment.

11. **Master Number 22: The Master Builder:**

• Associated Traits: Vision, practicality, mastery.

• Significance: Master Number 22 is a master builder, influencing traits of visionary thinking, practical skills, and the ability to manifest ideas into reality.

In 'The Secret Language of Birthdays April Profiles,' we explore how these specific numbers weave into your birthdate, creating a unique tapestry of traits that shape the essence of who you are. Get ready to embrace the significance of each number and uncover the extraordinary qualities they contribute to your personality!

Dive into the four astrological elements: Fire, Earth, Air, and Water.

Let's take a plunge into the captivating world of the four astrological elements—Fire, Earth, Air, and Water—in 'The Secret Language of Birthdays April Profiles.' Each element brings its own unique energy, shaping distinct traits and characteristics in individuals born under their influence.

1. **Fire Signs (Aries, Leo, Sagittarius):**

- **Energetic Essence:** Fire signs are dynamic, passionate, and full of vitality.

- **Traits:** Enthusiasm, creativity, courage, and a desire for adventure.

- **Influence:** The fire element ignites a spark of inspiration, driving these signs to pursue their passions with zeal and confidence.

2. **Earth Signs (Taurus, Virgo, Capricorn):**

- **Grounded Foundation:** Earth signs are practical, reliable, and grounded.

• **Traits:** Stability, patience, diligence, and a strong sense of responsibility.

• **Influence:** The earth element provides a solid foundation, shaping individuals who are realistic, hardworking, and deeply connected to the material world.

3. Air Signs (Gemini, Libra, Aquarius):

• **Intellectual Air:** Air signs are intellectual, communicative, and often sociable.

• **Traits:** Curiosity, adaptability, communication skills, and a love for social interactions.

• **Influence:** The air element fosters a mental agility, shaping individuals who thrive on ideas, communication, and social connections.

4. Water Signs (Cancer, Scorpio, Pisces):

• **Emotional Depth:** Water signs are intuitive, emotional, and deeply connected to their feelings.

• **Traits:** Compassion, empathy, creativity, and a strong sense of intuition.

• **Influence:** The water element infuses a rich emotional depth, shaping individuals who are attuned to their inner world and often possess a nurturing and empathetic nature.

In 'The Secret Language of Birthdays April Profiles,' we explore how the astrological elements blend with your birthdate, creating a unique cosmic recipe for your personality. Whether you're ignited by the fire's passion, grounded in the earth's stability, soaring with the air's intellect, or flowing with the water's emotions, these elements play a key role in defining the essence of who you are. Get ready to embrace the elemental magic that shapes your individuality!

Discuss how each element contributes to personality traits.

Let's delve into the fascinating realm of how each astrological element contributes to personality traits in 'The Secret Language of Birthdays April Profiles.' Whether you're ignited by the passionate fire, grounded in the stability of earth, soaring with the intellect of air, or flowing with the emotions of water, each element brings its unique flavor to shape your individuality.

1. **Fire Signs (Aries, Leo, Sagittarius):**

• **Contributions to Personality:**

• **Passion:** Fire signs are known for their passionate and dynamic nature. They approach life with enthusiasm and energy.

• **Courage:** The fire element instills courage, empowering individuals to take risks and embrace challenges.

• **Creativity:** Fire signs often express themselves creatively, fueled by their vibrant and bold personalities.

2. **Earth Signs (Taurus, Virgo, Capricorn):**

• **Contributions to Personality:**

• **Stability:** Earth signs bring a sense of stability and reliability to their personalities. They are practical and grounded.

• **Diligence:** The earth element instills a strong work ethic and a diligent approach to tasks and responsibilities.

• **Material Connection:** Earth signs are often connected to the material world, valuing security and tangible achievements.

3. **Air Signs (Gemini, Libra, Aquarius):**

• **Contributions to Personality:**

• **Intellect:** Air signs are intellectually oriented, valuing ideas, communication, and mental pursuits.

• **Adaptability:** The air element fosters adaptability, making individuals open to new perspectives and ideas.

• **Social Skills:** Air signs excel in social interactions, possessing effective communication skills and a love for social connections.

4. **Water Signs (Cancer, Scorpio, Pisces):**

• **Contributions to Personality:**

• **Emotional Depth:** Water signs are deeply connected to their emotions, fostering empathy and a rich inner life.

• **Intuition:** The water element enhances intuition, making individuals perceptive and attuned to subtle energies.

• **Creativity:** Water signs often channel their emotions into creative endeavors, expressing themselves through art and imagination.

In 'The Secret Language of Birthdays April Profiles,' we explore how the combination of your birthdate and these astrological elements creates a personalized cosmic profile. Whether you find resonance in the fiery passion, the grounded stability, the intellectual air, or the emotional depth of water, each element contributes to the mosaic of your personality. Get ready to embrace the elemental dance that shapes the essence of who you are!

Astrological Profile for Those Born on April 1

If your birthday falls on April 1, you are a vibrant Aries, guided by the influential forces of Mars and the Sun. This cosmic duo bestows upon you an undeniable creative prowess and an irresistible charm that captivates those around you. Your knack for selecting the most exquisite attire reflects your desire to leave a lasting impression, reinforcing your role as a natural-born leader.

As a charismatic individual, people naturally look up to you, drawn by your magnetic aura. It's essential, however, to wield the respect and authority bestowed upon you with care, avoiding any temptation to misuse such positions. Balancing the potent energy of your ego urges becomes crucial, as mastering this art allows you to leverage your prominence for personal growth and extend assistance to others—an ideal win-win scenario.

April 1st births mark the beginning of a journey fueled by ambition and a quest for perfection in every endeavor. While your passion fuels your work, it also propels you toward taking calculated risks, though sometimes these ventures may lead to unforeseen outcomes. This day is often associated with visions of family, love, and financial prosperity, with a generous spirit characterizing those born on this date. It's advisable to maintain realistic expectations in your pursuits.

Individuals born on April 1 exhibit traits of openness, directness, and unwavering perseverance. Despite occasional impatience and restlessness, their sharp intellect positions them as valuable assets in leadership roles. Their sense of responsibility is commendable, aligning with their aptitude for effective leadership.

Driven by ambition, April 1st individuals are not afraid to go the extra mile to achieve their goals. Their readiness to assume leadership positions is complemented by a keen awareness of the associated responsibilities and consequences. Love comes early and profoundly for them, often resulting in early marriages once they feel ready to embark on such significant life milestones.

Astrological Nuggets for April 1 Birthdays:

• **Lucky Colors:** Embrace the allure of copper and gold to enhance your positive energy.

• **Lucky Gem:** Adorn yourself with the regal ruby to attract prosperity and good fortune.

• **Fortunate Days:** Bask in the cosmic energy on Sunday, Monday, and Thursday for optimal outcomes.

• **Numbers for Success:** Navigate through life's changes with confidence by recognizing the significance of 1, 10, 19, 28, 37, 46, 55, 64, 73, and 82.

Notable Individuals Sharing Your Birthday: Celebrate your April 1st birthday alongside the likes of Lon Chaney, Debbie Reynolds, Hannah Spearritt, Sam Huntington, and Tavares Cherry. Each of these figures contributes to the rich tapestry of individuals born on this remarkable date, sharing in the unique qualities and cosmic influences that shape their journeys.

Embrace your cosmic identity, and may each passing year bring new adventures, personal growth, and an abundance of joy on your April 1st journey through life.

Extended Astrological Profile for Those Born on April 2

Born under the radiant influence of Aries with Mars and the Moon as your personal ruling planets, if your birthday falls on April 2, you embody a captivating blend of emotional depth and artistic flair. Your love for people is expressed through your ever-changing emotions, occasionally veering into moodiness. However, this emotional rollercoaster only adds to your endearing nature, making you magnetic to those around you.

While you possess a sincere desire to be liked by everyone, it's essential to navigate the fine line between seeking approval and staying true to yourself. Your artistic inclinations align you with the realms of musicians, authors, and artists, suggesting a natural affinity for the aesthetic and imaginative. Your high level of imagination and idealism marks you as a dreamer who finds solace in the realms of fantasy and creative expression.

Managing your personal and domestic space becomes crucial for you, providing a foundation for your artistic and empathetic endeavors. Your ability to work with large groups is grounded in your caring and empathetic nature, but it's equally important to channel your fiery emotions constructively.

Astrological Traits and Elements: Ruled by the fiery element, you exude enthusiasm and flexibility, akin to the transformative nature of fire molding the earth. Tuesday, associated with activity and hope, is your designated day, infusing your life with energy and forward-thinking. The lucky numbers 7, 8, 13, 20, and 26 further define the nuances of your cosmic connection, guiding your interactions with others.

Personality Traits: April 2 individuals are imaginative, outgoing, and diplomatic, equipped with a creative and analytical mind that propels them into effective leadership roles. Their open-mindedness and honest disposition make them amiable individuals with a penchant for solving problems independently. While they harbor a desire for freedom and independence, they need to balance these traits to avoid reticence in relationships.

Health and Relationships: Individuals born on April 2 generally experience mild emotional swings, contributing to harmonious family dynamics. Their ability to recover quickly from illness and work effectively in partnerships underscores their balanced approach to health and relationships.

Inventive and Creative: April 2 individuals boast an inventive and creative streak, coupled with a natural eye for the unusual. These qualities make them attractive to others, enhancing their appeal in partnerships. While loyalty may not be their strongest suit, a wide circle of friends contributes to their self-esteem.

Lucky Elements: Cream, white, and green are your lucky colors, infusing your life with positive energy. Moonstone or pearl serves as your lucky gem, enhancing your connection to the cosmic forces. Mondays, Thursdays, and Sundays are your fortuitous days of the week, aligning with your cosmic energies.

Fortunate Numbers: Navigate the waves of change with confidence, recognizing the significance of the numbers 2, 11, 20, 29, 38, 47, 56, 65, and 74.

Notable Individuals Sharing Your Birthday: Celebrate your April 2nd birthday alongside iconic figures such as Casanova, Hans Christian Anderson, Emile Zola, Alec Guinness, Jack Webb, and Joie

Lenz. These individuals contribute to the tapestry of personalities born on this remarkable date, sharing in the cosmic influences that shape their unique journeys.

As you continue your cosmic journey, may your artistic endeavors flourish, your relationships prosper, and each passing year bring new adventures and personal growth on your April 2nd path through life.

Astrological Profile for Those Born on April 3

If your birthday graces the date of April 3, you are an Aries, guided by the influential forces of Mars and Jupiter. The auspicious Jupiter takes the lead, reflecting your moral and spiritual nature. High standards, integrity, and fair play define your character, exhibiting empathy, compassion, and a genuine concern for all. Coupled with good executive ability, your well-balanced judgment, honesty, and self-confidence contribute to the jovial and exuberant spirit that defines you.

Spiritual Awakening and Inner Journeys: Under the combined influence of Venus and Jupiter, long journeys are indicated, not just in the physical realm but also on a mental or spiritual plane. Your path may lead to inner awakening and mystical experiences, fostering a fascination with the unknown. Inner growth and spiritual enlightenment are potential milestones on your journey, reflecting the depth of your introspective nature.

Ambition and Foresight: Born on April 3, you possess foresight and ambition that guide your life's decisions from an early age. This innate ambition fosters focus, enabling you to make informed decisions and set clear goals for yourself. Your dreams, wild and spontaneous, provide insights into your future path, contributing to your overall sense of purpose and direction.

Strengths and Leadership Traits: Your well-developed intuition allows you to delve into the core of problems, and your ability to express opinions clearly makes you an instructive presence. Physical strength further adds to your arsenal, making you an excellent leader. Despite occasional stubbornness, your ability to learn from errors contributes to your overall strength and resilience.

Career Ambitions and Enthusiasm: In your professional realm, enthusiasm drives your interest in careers where quick financial gains are possible. A desire to help others coupled with insights into their needs shapes your career choices. Ambition and drive are prominent features, propelling you toward success in endeavors that align with your goals.

Love and Romance: In matters of love and romance, the April 3 native of Aries is an exciting and dynamic partner. Your charismatic and passionate nature contributes to the magnetic attraction you hold in relationships. As an Aries, your love life is infused with energy, enthusiasm, and a natural ability to create excitement in the romantic sphere.

Lucky Elements: Yellow, lemon, and sandy shades are your lucky colors, infusing your life with positive energy. Adorn yourself with the vibrant yellow sapphire, citrine quartz, or golden topaz as your lucky gems. Thursdays, Sundays, and Tuesdays are your fortuitous days of the week, aligning with your cosmic energies.

Fortunate Numbers: Navigate the waves of change with confidence, recognizing the significance of the numbers 3, 12, 21, 30, 39, 48, 57, 66, and 75.

Notable Individuals Sharing Your Birthday: Celebrate your April 3rd birthday alongside esteemed figures such as Washington Irving, George Jessel, Marlon Brando, Doris Day, Wayne Newton, Alec Baldwin, and Eddie Murphy. These individuals contribute to the tapestry of personalities born on this remarkable date, sharing in the cosmic influences that shape their unique journeys.

As you continue your cosmic journey, may the auspicious alignment of Mars and Jupiter guide you towards personal growth, spiritual enlightenment, and the fulfillment of your ambitions on your April 3rd path through life.

Astrological Profile for Those Born on April 4

Born under the dynamic influence of Aries with Mars and Uranus as your personal ruling planets, if your birthday falls on April 4, you possess a methodical thought process that demands a balance between your opinions and consideration for others' viewpoints. Your hardworking nature may lead you to exceed physical capacities, resulting in self-criticism. The number 4 emphasizes a strong desire for material success, urging you to find harmony between worldly pursuits and inner spiritual life.

Personality Traits and Eccentricity: April 4 brings a unique set of personality traits, marked by eccentricity and a penchant for the unusual. Creativity, innovation, and natural inspiration define individuals born on this day, with potential benefits or challenges depending on their application in daily life. The Aries modality underscores initiative, novelty, and individual selfhood, guiding your approach to various aspects of life.

Risk and Self-Control: Aries' high-risk association with injuries and accidents serves as a cautionary note, urging individuals born on April 4 to exercise self-control and mindfulness. Striking a balance between assertiveness and humility is crucial, avoiding excessive bossiness or haughtiness. Optimism and self-belief play key roles in navigating the challenges associated with this birthday.

Emotional Expression and Relationships: Expressing emotions may pose a challenge for those born on April 4, requiring honesty and healthy outlets for emotional release. The tendency towards egotism and impulsiveness is counterbalanced by loyalty, intelligence, and charm. Relationships with April 4 individuals are characterized by their easy-going nature, making them pleasant companions.

Lucky Elements: Electric blue, electric white, and multi-colors are your lucky colors, infusing your life with vibrant energy. Hessonite garnet and agate serve as your lucky gems, enhancing your connection to cosmic forces. Sundays and Tuesdays are your fortuitous days of the week, aligning with your cosmic energies.

Fortunate Numbers: Navigate the waves of change with confidence, recognizing the significance of the numbers 4, 13, 22, 31, 40, 49, 58, 67, and 76.

Notable Individuals Sharing Your Birthday: Celebrate your April 4th birthday alongside esteemed figures such as Arthur Murray, Muddy Waters, Elmer Bernstein, Anthony Perkins, Robert Downey Jr., Heath Ledger, and Isabelle Brinkman. Each of these individuals contributes to the rich tapestry of personalities born on this remarkable date, sharing in the cosmic influences that shape their unique journeys.

As you traverse the cosmic landscape guided by Mars and Uranus, may your methodical approach blend harmoniously with your creative spirit, fostering personal growth, spiritual enlightenment, and material success on your April 4th path through life.

Astrological Profile for Those Born on April 5

Born under the vibrant influence of Aries with Mars and Mercury as your personal ruling planets, if your birthday falls on April 5, you possess an invigorating blend of swiftness, curiosity, and inventiveness. Mercury's presence adds a zing to your nature, fueling a perpetual quest for understanding the whys and wherefores of everything. Your dynamic energy propels you into constant motion, prompting a reminder to find moments of stillness amid the ceaseless movement.

Intellectual Agility and Inventiveness: Mercury's influence endows you with incredible mental agility, making you swift and curious by nature. Inventiveness characterizes your approach to challenges, and you thrive in studious and intellectual spheres. The capacity to absorb information is a prominent aspect of your nature, positioning you well in industries that demand intellectual prowess.

Eternal Youthfulness and Family Love: Despite your perpetual motion, a love for family and children shines through, and your nature remains forever youthful. Reliability and hard work define your character, contributing to your success in endeavors that align with your ambitions.

Ambition and Leadership: Individuals born on April 5 are highly ambitious, displaying eagerness to lead and make decisions. The initiative-taking nature is balanced by a preference for self-direction, and you excel in activities that allow you to showcase your talents and shine. A charming and sociable demeanor, combined with a harmonious blend of logic and creativity, makes you effective in both personal and professional relationships.

Resourcefulness and Industriousness: Resourcefulness, industriousness, and a drive for accomplishment characterize your approach to life. The perpetual need for activity stems from a deep-seated ambition that propels you forward. While you focus on results, there's an acknowledgment of subtler sources of satisfaction that contribute to your holistic well-being.

Planetary Alignment and Practical Achievements: The conjunction of Mars and Pluto on April 5 signifies a time of positive accomplishment. Practicality guides your decisions, emphasizing what is important in life and deriving joy from achieving meaningful goals. However, caution is advised to avoid inadvertently antagonizing others. Harness the practical energy to act positively and await favorable events before taking decisive actions.

Lucky Elements: Green is your lucky color, symbolizing growth, balance, and vitality. Adorn yourself with Emerald, Aquamarine, or Jade, as these gems enhance your connection to positive cosmic energies. Wednesdays, Fridays, and Saturdays are your fortuitous days of the week, aligning with your cosmic rhythm.

Fortunate Numbers: Navigate the waves of change with confidence, recognizing the significance of the numbers 5, 14, 23, 32, 41, 50, 59, 68, and 77.

Notable Individuals Sharing Your Birthday: Celebrate your April 5th birthday alongside esteemed figures such as Thomas Hobbes, Algernon Swinburne, Spencer Tracy, Bette Davis, Gregory Peck, Krista Allen, and Michael Moriarty. Each of these individuals contributes to the rich tapestry of personalities born on this remarkable date, sharing in the cosmic influences that shape their unique journeys.

May the dynamic blend of Mars and Mercury guide you towards intellectual achievements, familial love, and practical success on your April 5th path through life.

Astrological Profile for Those Born on April 6

Harmony and Love-Powered Ambition: If your birthday falls on April 6, you embody the vibrant spirit of Aries, with the influential forces of Mars and Venus shaping your astrological profile. Governed by the Planet of Love, Venus, your pursuits reflect a drive for both worldly success and fulfillment in personal relationships. The qualities of love, sympathy, and harmony are woven into the fabric of your personality, bringing forth refined and aesthetic pleasures in art, poetry, and beauty.

Agreeable Personality and Relationship Dynamics: Your agreeable nature is marked by a strong desire to maintain friendships, even when relationships may have outworn their significance. It is vital to learn the art of letting go, releasing connections that no longer add value to your life. With a strong attraction to the opposite sex, admirers are never in short supply.

Passionate Intelligence and Aggressive Energy: Individuals born on April 6th are characterized by passion, intelligence, and a touch of aggression. While you make excellent friends, navigating relationships may present challenges. Expect a plethora of friendships and be prepared for relationship complexities. Your uncontrollable desire for the best in life fuels your pursuit of harmony in every aspect, and offenses to your sensibilities can be unsettling.

Financial Responsibility and Creative Strengths: Navigating financial waters can be tricky, as you may struggle with money management but harbor an intense sense of financial responsibility. Your creative nature serves as a strength, and effective communication of your ideas is crucial. Resist the temptation to spend excessively, and maintain a balance between passion and practicality.

Leadership Traits and Team Dynamics: April 6 individuals are often seen as good leaders, driven by a strong desire for autonomy and a keen eye for detail. Your value as a team player lies in your ability to solve problems, though stubbornness, impatience, and moodiness may be occasional challenges. Your optimism, open-mindedness, and commitment to personal growth make you an asset in various endeavors.

Lucky Elements: Embrace the fortunate energies associated with white and cream, rose and pink. Diamond, white sapphire, or quartz crystal serve as your lucky gems, enhancing your connection to positive cosmic forces. Fridays, Saturdays, and Wednesdays are your auspicious days, aligning with the cosmic rhythm that guides your path.

Numbers and Years of Change: Navigate the waves of transformation with confidence, acknowledging the importance of the numbers 6, 15, 24, 33, 42, 51, 60, 69, and 78.

Notable Individuals Sharing Your Birthday: Celebrate your April 6th birthday alongside esteemed figures such as Lowell Thomas, Richard Alpert (Baba Ram Dass), Merle Haggard, Ari Meyers, Bret Boone, and Candace Cameron. Each of these individuals contributes to the rich tapestry of personalities born on this remarkable date, sharing in the cosmic influences that shape their unique journeys.

May the harmonious interplay of Mars and Venus guide you towards success in both worldly pursuits and fulfilling relationships as you navigate the dynamic path of life.

Extended Astrological Profile for Those Born on April 7

Neptune's Mystical Influence: If your birthday falls on April 7, your astrological profile is infused with the ethereal energy of Aries, guided by the mystical Neptune alongside the fiery Mars. Neptune's influence mirrors the vastness of the ocean, rendering you restless, moody, and enamored with change and travel. Your affinity for water and sea-connected places reflects the profound impact of Neptune on your nature.

Unconventional Ideas and Compassionate Spirit: Possessing unique and original ideas in the realms of religion and philosophy, you exhibit compassion elevated to sublime heights. Your willingness to go to any lengths to help those in need highlights a profound sense of empathy. However, maintaining balance in addressing your own needs is crucial to avoid becoming a victim of the very people you seek to assist.

Financial Wisdom for Material Success: As indicated by your Birthday Horoscope on April 7, embracing lessons in financial economy is essential for optimal material results. Balancing your compassionate nature with practical financial wisdom ensures stability and prosperity on the material plane.

Intelligence, Sensitivity, and Adaptability: Your intelligence, responsiveness, creativity, and heightened sensitivity to energy define your multifaceted personality. Quick adaptability to change is a notable strength, and your potential for leadership spans across various fields. While your friendly and charming demeanor endears you to friends, maintaining a degree of independence and solitude is crucial for processing thoughts and fostering freedom.

Impulsivity, Adventure, and Jealousy in Love: Aries' influence can bring forth impulsivity and a penchant for adventure. In love, your considerate and nice demeanor is accompanied by a touch of jealousy. Balancing passion and a sense of security in relationships becomes key to maintaining harmony.

Communication Skills and Leadership Potential: Your excellent communication skills may draw you towards management positions or entrepreneurship. Leadership roles that present challenges align well with your innovative and creative spirit. Success in new endeavors or recognition through awards is within reach with the right motivation.

Lucky Elements: Embrace the darker green shades as your lucky colors, resonating with the mysteries of Neptune's influence. Turquoise, cat's eye chrysoberyl, and tiger's eye stand as your lucky gems, channeling positive energies. Mondays and Thursdays are your auspicious days, providing favorable alignments.

Numbers and Years of Change: Navigate through transformative phases with the vibrations of the numbers 7, 16, 25, 34, 43, 52, 61, 70, and 79.

Notable Individuals Sharing Your Birthday: Celebrate your April 7th birthday alongside renowned figures such as William Wordsworth, Walter Winchell, Billie Holiday, David Frost, Francis Ford Coppola, Jackie Chan, and Russell Crowe. Each of these individuals contributes to the rich tapestry of personalities born on this captivating date, sharing in the cosmic influences that shape their unique journeys.

May the interplay of Aries' fiery determination and Neptune's mystical currents guide you toward a harmonious blend of spiritual depth and material success on your cosmic voyage.

Astrological Profile for Those Born on April 8

Balancing Pessimism with Optimism: Born under the influence of Aries with Mars and Saturn as your personal ruling planets, individuals with an April 8 birthday exude ambition, resourcefulness, and prudence. While you display a strong sense of purpose, there may be moments when a veil of pessimism clouds your perspective. Balancing this tendency with joy, optimism, and inner sunshine can pave the way for better results in various aspects of life.

Financial Acumen and Strong Ambition: Your proficiency with money and a highly resourceful nature are evident traits, enhancing your practical dealings and financial wisdom. A solid sense of purpose, coupled with ambition, forms the foundation for success in your endeavors. However, it's essential to strike a balance and not lose sight of life's other dimensions beyond work.

The Practical, Ambitious, and Emotional Aries: People born on April 8 are characterized by their impatience, ambition, and aggression. Remarkably capable of making important decisions, they demonstrate practicality and orderliness in their approach to life. While they may come across as greedy, their financial savvy and strong sense of purpose contribute to their success.

Emotionally, you possess a compassionate nature, seeking to share your life with others and prioritizing their well-being. This emotional depth, however, may lead to intolerance towards differing views.

Managing strong opinions with an open mind can foster harmonious relationships.

Relationship Dynamics and Authority Figure Role: In relationships, those born on April 8 are drawn to individuals with a growth mindset. Direct and forthright, you seek long-term connections but may need to navigate unrealistic expectations and naivety. The role of the "authority figure" often emerges in your relationships, reflecting a sense of responsibility developed early in life.

Balancing Work and Life: While diligence and a strong work ethic characterize your professional approach, it's essential to remember that life extends beyond work. Embracing a quiet hobby that allows for moments of peace and quiet can provide a necessary counterbalance to your industrious endeavors.

Lucky Elements: Deep blue and black stand as your lucky colors, resonating with the profound and authoritative aspects of your personality. Blue sapphire, lapis lazuli, and amethyst emerge as your lucky gems, aligning with your astrological influences. Wednesdays, Fridays, and Saturdays are your fortunate days, contributing positive energies to your endeavors.

Numbers and Years of Change: Navigate transformative phases with the vibrational energies of the numbers 8, 17, 26, 35, 44, 53, 62, and 71.

Notable Individuals Sharing Your Birthday: Celebrate your April 8 birthday alongside esteemed personalities such as Patricia Arquette, Robin Wright Penn, Mary Pickford, and Kirsten Storms. Each of these individuals shares in the cosmic influences shaping their unique paths, contributing to the rich tapestry of Aries-born personalities.

May the alignment of Mars and Saturn guide you towards a harmonious blend of ambition, financial wisdom, and emotional depth on your cosmic journey.

Astrological Profile for Those Born on April 9

Mars Energy and Active Nature: As an Aries born on April 9, your astrological profile is shaped by the bold and energetic influence of Mars. This celestial force bestows upon you an active, passionate, and impulsive nature. Laziness finds no place in your world, as you excel in both work and physical activities. The double energy of Mars, however, brings forth traits of aggression, ruthlessness, and occasional insensitivity. Balancing this intensity with compromise and humility in relationships serves as a vital life lesson.

Creative and Witty, Seeking Self-Confidence: Individuals born on April 9 possess a high degree of creativity and wit. Despite these strengths, a potential lack of self-confidence and assertiveness may be observed. Nurturing your creative streak can foster relaxation and clearer thinking, enabling better decision-making. Recognize your knack for influencing others but be cautious not to misuse this trait for control.

Goal-Oriented Aries with Business Acumen: Aries individuals, including those born on April 9, embody a belief in the attainability of their goals and ideas. Your focus on practical application sets you apart, making you adept at turning ideas into real-life achievements. Goals often revolve around acquiring new skills or knowledge, and your strong business sense positions you as a capable investor.

Lucky Elements: Red, maroon, scarlet, and autumn tones align with the fiery energy of Mars, serving as your lucky colors. Red coral and garnet stand as auspicious gems, enhancing your astrological influences. Mondays, Tuesdays, and Thursdays are your fortunate days, providing positive energies for your endeavors.

Numbers and Years of Change: Navigate transformative phases with the vibrational energies of the numbers 9, 18, 27, 36, 45, 54, 63, and 72.

Notable Individuals Sharing Your Birthday: Celebrate your April 9 birthday alongside esteemed personalities such as Pierre C. Baudelaire, Mance Lipscomb, James W. Fulbright, Hugh Hefner, Jean-Paul Belmondo, Dennis Quaid, and Rachel Stevens. Each of these individuals, born under the influence of Mars, contributes to the diverse tapestry of Aries-born characteristics.

May the active and passionate energy of Mars guide you toward balanced relationships, creative expression, and the realization of your goals on your unique cosmic journey.

Astrological Profile for Those Born on April 10

Mars and Sun Influences: As an Aries born on April 10, your astrological profile is shaped by the dynamic interplay of Mars and the Sun. The amplified solar vibrations on your birthdate endow you with exceptional power and robust health. Your recuperative abilities are strong, complemented by heightened creative and communicative faculties. The Wheel of Fortune, represented by the number ten, indicates that success is not just a possibility but an inevitable outcome in your life.

Daredevil Spirit and Strong Ego: A daredevil at heart, you exhibit an unusual taste for tempting fate. With a potent ego and a keen sense of your own destiny, you naturally gravitate toward the limelight, making yourself the center of attention. Embracing the strength and weaknesses inherent in your April 10 birth, you can navigate life with honesty and realism, relying on the dependable and devoted qualities of the Aries sign.

Emotional Intensity and Romantic Passion: Born on April 10, your life is marked by intense emotions, urging caution against hasty decisions. The Aries romantic and passionate nature finds expression in your relationships, where you prioritize your partner and resist the allure of monotony. Affectionate, smart, and playful, you actively seek dynamic and engaging connections.

Career Opportunities and Leadership Traits: Your Aries strengths open up numerous opportunities, particularly in your career and personal life. A natural leader and advocate for change, you can shine brightly by embracing your strengths rather than fixating on flaws. The pursuit of approval from others is unnecessary for your happiness, as your inherent strengths pave the way for success.

Lucky Elements: Copper and gold are your lucky colors, resonating with the vibrant energy of your birth date. Ruby stands as your auspicious gem, enhancing your astrological influences. Sundays, Mondays, and Thursdays are considered lucky days, aligning with the favorable energies surrounding you. Embrace the vibrational powers of the numbers 1, 10, 19, 28, 37, 46, 55, 64, 73, and 82 during important phases of change.

Notable Individuals Sharing Your Birthday: Celebrate your April 10 birthday alongside esteemed personalities such as A.E. (G.W. Russell), Chuck Connors, Omar Sharif, Steven Seagal, Michael Pitt, Mandy Moore, and Ryan Merriman. Each of these individuals, born under the influential combination of Mars and the Sun, contributes to the diverse tapestry of Aries-born characteristics.

May the powerful blend of Mars and the Sun guide you towards success, passion, and dynamic relationships on your unique cosmic journey.

Astrological Profile for Those Born on April 11

Mars and Moon Energies: As an Aries born on April 11, your astrological profile is governed by the potent influences of Mars and the Moon. A social and dynamic individual, you embody the characteristics of your ruling planets, balancing a spirited enthusiasm with emotional depth. While your social nature shines brightly, moments of impatience and restlessness may arise. Harnessing the fire of your spirit creatively can redirect these energies, preventing the frustration of banging your head against obstacles.

Innate Love of Sharing and Responsibilities: A natural inclination towards sharing and a desire for fair rewards for your efforts characterize your personality. However, the tendency to take on excessive tasks and responsibilities may pose challenges. Balancing your workload and prioritizing tasks is essential for your well-being.

Creative and Multifaceted Nature: The April 11 birthday personality is marked by creativity and multifaceted talents. However, the potential for feeling depressed arises when expectations fall short. Prioritizing projects becomes crucial for avoiding overwhelm and unlocking your full potential. Embracing your multifaceted nature can lead to personal fulfillment.

Love and Success Through Travel: Individuals born on April 11 often encounter challenges in matters of love and long-term relationships. The key lies in prioritizing and finding ways to navigate through these difficulties. Travel can play a significant role in the life of an April 11 individual, potentially leading to great love or success.

Emotional Charged Times: The April 11 birthday horoscope highlights the importance of acting during opportune moments, acknowledging the emotionally charged nature of these times. Juggling multiple projects may cloud the consequences of decisions, emphasizing the need for focused attention.

Strength Through Empathy and Compassion: Your empathetic and compassionate nature positions you as a natural mediator and leader. The ability to find common ground in your career and social interactions makes you a valuable asset in group dynamics. While socializing and participating in events are enjoyable, allowing time for personal unwinding is essential.

Lucky Elements: Cream, white, and green are your lucky colors, resonating with the harmonious energies surrounding your birth. Moonstone or pearl serve as auspicious gems, enhancing the positive vibrations in your life. Mondays, Thursdays, and Sundays are considered lucky days, aligning with the favorable influences that accompany these times. Numbers such as 2, 11, 20, 29, 38, 47, 56, 65, and 74 hold significance in your journey, especially during pivotal moments of change.

Notable Individuals Sharing Your Birthday: Celebrate your April 11 birthday alongside notable individuals such as Charles Evans Hughes, Jennifer Esposito, Josh Server, Allessandra Ambrosio, and Cerys Matthews. Each person born on this day contributes to the rich tapestry of Aries personalities, embodying the dynamic interplay of Mars and the Moon.

May your journey be filled with creative fulfillment, harmonious relationships, and the successful navigation of life's challenges.

Astrological Profile for Those Born on April 12

Mars and Jupiter Energies: Born under the influence of Mars and Jupiter, your Aries personality is characterized by high ideals, big plans, and strong ambitions. However, your astrological profile suggests the need to soften demands on others, avoiding potential disappointments due to unmet expectations. Your friends and colleagues may struggle to keep up with your aspirations, which could stem from a deep-seated need for approval.

Contentment with Self: The advice from the stars encourages you to find contentment within yourself. Recognize that you are your strongest and most valuable asset. While resistance to your deepest desires may surface, this trait can serve you well in shaping a positive future. Embracing your individuality and learning to be content with your own self can lead to greater fulfillment.

Magnetic Influence and Conflict Resolution: Your magnetic personality is a source of attraction, allowing you to create change and overcome challenges. The ability to unify warring groups and focus on conflict resolution positions you as a great teacher. Your deep compassion contributes to your success in various situations.

Organized, Healthy, and Positive: Individuals born on April 12 are generally well-organized, maintaining good health and a positive outlook on life. Trustworthy and trusting, they exhibit enthusiasm and creativity, making them suitable for leadership roles or middle management. However, setbacks may arise, including the potential for accidents or upper-body problems.

Challenges in Romantic Relationships: April 12th individuals may encounter challenges in romantic relationships. Radical steps or activism could lead to threats or attacks, urging caution in such endeavors. The quest for a trustworthy partner may be challenging for these passionate and free-spirited individuals, possibly resulting in experiences of unrequited affection.

Lucky Elements: Yellow, lemon, and sandy shades are your lucky colors, resonating with positive energies surrounding your birth. Yellow sapphire, citrine quartz, and golden topaz serve as auspicious gems, enhancing the favorable vibrations in your life. Thursdays, Sundays, and Tuesdays are considered lucky days, aligning with the beneficial influences that accompany these times. Numbers such as 3, 12, 21, 30, 39, 48, 57, 66, and 75 hold significance in your journey, especially during pivotal moments of change.

Notable Individuals Sharing Your Birthday: Celebrate your April 12 birthday alongside notable individuals such as David Cassidy, David Letterman, Andy Garcia, Shannen Doherty, Claire Danes, and Jelena Dokic. Each person born on this day contributes to the diverse tapestry of Aries personalities, embodying the dynamic interplay of Mars and Jupiter.

May your journey be marked by self-contentment, magnetic influence, and successful conflict resolution. Embrace your unique qualities and navigate the challenges of relationships with wisdom and resilience.

Astrological Profile for Those Born on April 13

Mars and Uranus Energies: As an Aries born on April 13, your astrological profile is influenced by the dynamic combination of Mars and Uranus. This planetary alignment imparts a sense of constant movement, change, and unexpected eruptions in your life. Just when you anticipate a sense of settling down, life throws another curveball. The advice from the stars encourages you to consider planning more carefully to bring about a secure and predictable outcome.

Life Lesson: Controlling Emotions and Expressing Frustrations: Your life lesson revolves around mastering the art of controlling emotions while still expressing frustrations. The energetic and unpredictable nature of Mars and Uranus within you can lead to intense emotions and sudden outbursts. Learning to navigate these emotional currents with poise and expressing frustrations constructively will contribute to personal growth.

Reformer and Unconventional Problem Solver: People born on April 13 are recognized as reformers and unconventional problem solvers. Your high energy levels and constant movement make you prone to seeking new solutions and approaches. While you thrive on dynamic situations, being alone may not bring out your best ideas. Collaboration, mentorship, and openness to learning new concepts can enhance your problem-solving abilities.

Strong Morals and Desire for Love: Individuals born on April 13 possess strong morals and a deep desire for love. Lack of love may lead to emotional struggles, emphasizing the importance of cultivating meaningful relationships. Despite the potential for emotional turmoil, your resilience and active mindset allow you to continually work towards happiness. The relentless pursuit of creative endeavors becomes a powerful means of dealing with contradictions in life.

Confident and Assertive Leadership Skills: April 13th individuals exhibit confidence, assertiveness, and strong leadership skills. Your bold and outspoken nature enables you to take on tasks that others may shy away from. This day is marked by a natural ability to manage people and projects, contributing to your success in leadership roles.

Lucky Elements: Electric blue, electric white, and multi-colors are your lucky colors, resonating with positive energies surrounding your birth. Hessonite garnet and agate serve as auspicious gems, enhancing the favorable vibrations in your life. Sundays and Tuesdays are considered lucky days, aligning with the beneficial influences that accompany these times. Numbers such as 4, 13, 22, 31, 40, 49, 58, 67, and 76 hold significance in your journey, especially during pivotal moments of change.

Notable Individuals Sharing Your Birthday: Celebrate your April 13 birthday alongside notable individuals such as Thomas Jefferson, Samuel Beckett, Caroline Rhea, Rick Schroder, and Sylvie Meis. Each person born on this day contributes to the diverse tapestry of Aries personalities, embodying the dynamic interplay of Mars and Uranus.

May your journey be marked by careful planning, emotional mastery, and innovative problem-solving. Embrace the reformer within you and channel your dynamic energy into positive creative pursuits.

Astrological Profile for Those Born on April 14

Mars and Mercury Dynamics: As an Aries born on April 14, your astrological profile is shaped by the influential combination of Mars and Mercury. This unique alignment gives you a distinctive, if not forceful, manner of expressing yourself. Your quick wit and humorous streak have the power to disarm and influence those around you effectively. However, it's important to recognize that this forceful demeanor may overwhelm others at times. Be mindful of using your influential abilities judiciously to avoid alienating friends with trivial desires.

Health Considerations: The stars suggest a potential vulnerability in the throat area, advising you to pay attention to your breathing process and overall throat health. Being aware of this potential weakness can empower you to take proactive measures to maintain your well-being.

Family-Oriented and Empathic Nature: People born on April 14 often display a strong orientation towards family and possess a natural empathy. Curiosity for the unusual and a tendency to question various aspects of life characterize your approach. However, emotional rigidity may pose a challenge, especially when confronting changes and the aging process. Embracing flexibility and openness can contribute to a more harmonious emotional journey.

Cardinal Traits and Relationship Dynamics: April 14 birthdays are associated with the Cardinal zodiac sign, symbolizing love, orderliness, and reservation. The first house, representing initiative and individual uniqueness, further underscores your leadership qualities. Communication plays a pivotal role in your approach to love, and you may seek a partner who shares similar interests and beliefs. Your determination and ambition are prominent traits, making you well-suited for entrepreneurial ventures. While rebellious tendencies may surface, maintaining an open and learning-oriented mindset is essential for personal and professional growth.

Outgoing and Creative Traits: Individuals born on April 14 exhibit exceptional determination and ambition, often thriving in entrepreneurial roles and displaying risk-taking leadership. Despite occasional rebelliousness, you possess an outgoing and creative nature, excelling in social situations. Your ability to navigate social dynamics and communicate effectively contributes to your success in various interpersonal endeavors.

Lucky Elements: Green is considered your lucky color, representing balance, growth, and harmony. Emerald, Aquamarine, and Jade are your fortunate gems, enhancing positive energies in your life. Wednesdays, Fridays, and Saturdays are designated as lucky days, aligning with favorable cosmic influences. Numbers such as 5, 14, 23, 32, 41, 50, 59, 68, and 77 hold significance in your journey and mark important stages of change.

Notable Individuals Sharing Your Birthday: Celebrate your April 14 birthday alongside notable individuals such as Arnold Toynbee, Rod Steiger, Julie Christie, Els Tibau, Amy Dumas (Lita), and Sarah Michelle Gellar. Each person born on this day contributes to the diverse tapestry of Aries personalities, embodying the dynamic interplay of Mars and Mercury.

May your journey be marked by balanced influence, emotional openness, and successful ventures. Embrace your family-oriented nature, cultivate empathy, and utilize your determination to navigate the challenges and triumphs that come your way.

Astrological Profile for Those Born on April 15

Passionate and Dedicated Aries: Born on April 15, your astrological profile is defined by the dynamic influence of Mars and Venus. Passion is your hallmark, permeating every aspect of your life. Whether embarking on a project or navigating relationships, you approach endeavors with unwavering commitment, concentration, and dedication to your ideals. This passion extends to your charming and seductive nature, which you skillfully employ on your path to success.

Career and Relationship Dynamics: Your astrological alignment suggests that public relations, sales, or any profession requiring persuasive communication is well-suited to your strengths. The potential for marriage arising from your career pursuits is indicated, emphasizing the intertwining of personal and professional aspects of your life.

Impulsive Nature and Creative Talents: The birthday horoscope for April 15 individuals characterizes them as highly personal and energetic. Your impulsive nature, while a source of vitality, may also lead to attachments to unnecessary people or things. This inclination can make you gullible and unreliable at times. Channeling your innate creativity and multi-talented abilities can be a key to success, with potential interests spanning various fields such as science or law. Striking a balance between seriousness and relaxation is crucial for overcoming challenges and avoiding potential setbacks.

Vulnerability to Strong Rebuffs: While your talents are admired by pragmatic individuals in your life, the advice for those born on April 15 is to be less serious and more relaxed. This adjustment can mitigate potential vulnerability to strong rebuffs and enhance your overall resilience. Embracing a more lighthearted approach may prove beneficial in navigating both personal and professional spheres.

Taurus Influence and Selfish Tendencies: The influence of Taurus may manifest in a bit of selfishness, but the potential rewards make it worthwhile once your endeavors come to fruition. While understanding the viewpoints of others may be challenging for Taurus, embracing this perspective can present valuable opportunities for growth and collaboration.

Lucky Elements: White and cream, rose and pink are considered your lucky colors, reflecting themes of purity, passion, and balance. Diamond, white sapphire, or quartz crystal are your fortunate gems, enhancing positive energies in your life. Fridays, Saturdays, and Wednesdays are designated as lucky days, aligning with favorable cosmic influences. Numbers such as 6, 15, 24, 33, 42, 51, 60, 69, and 78 hold significance in your journey and mark important stages of change.

Notable Individuals Sharing Your Birthday: Celebrate your April 15 birthday alongside notable individuals such as Leonardo da Vinci, Henry James, Bessie Smith, Elizabeth Montgomery, Emma Thompson, Susan Ward, and Jessica Riddle. Each person born on this day contributes to the diverse tapestry of Aries personalities, embodying the unique interplay of Mars and Venus.

May your journey be marked by passionate pursuits, successful ventures, and harmonious relationships. Embrace the charm and dedication that define you, utilizing your persuasive skills to navigate both personal and professional endeavors with grace and determination.

In-Depth Astrological Profile for Those Born on April 16

Creative Vision and Practical Realism: Born under the Aries sign with Mars and Neptune as your personal ruling planets, you possess a unique blend of creativity and imagination. While Neptune endows you with high levels of creativity and a vivid imagination, you equally value the practical realization of your dreams. This dual influence allows you to bridge the gap between the ethereal and the material world, manifesting your creative visions into tangible realities. However, the intensity of your passion and creative visualization may pose challenges in relationships, with partners possibly feeling they are in competition with your imaginative dreams.

Relationship Dynamics and Sexual Power: For those born on April 16, maintaining a single relationship at a time is emphasized. It's essential to avoid using your sexual power as a means of control over others. Your sensitivity, compassion, and generosity define your approach to relationships, yet moments of aloofness and indifference may surface. Despite occasional naivety, you are forgiving and open to learning from mistakes, fostering positive attributes in your personality.

Positive Traits and Challenges: Your personality is marked by determination, diligence, and a willingness to take risks. Quick-witted and adept at overcoming challenges, you naturally attract friends and lovers with similar traits. While adventures and exciting experiences characterize your life, shyness or reserve may pose challenges in interpersonal interactions. The ambivalent relationship between career and individuals born on April 16 is evident, with a tendency to feel frustrated by obstacles. The pursuit of law and engineering may align with your talents, yet unfulfilled dreams can linger.

Money Matters and Communication: Effective communication about financial matters with loved ones is crucial. Disagreements in this realm may hinder progress, emphasizing the need for open and transparent discussions. Attractiveness alone does not guarantee goodness, prompting a deeper exploration of individuals' personality traits.

Lucky Elements: Your lucky colors include the darker shades of green, symbolizing growth, balance, and renewal. Turquoise, cat's eye chrysoberyl, and tiger's eye are your fortunate gems, aligning with the energies that bring stability and protection. Mondays and Thursdays are designated as your lucky days, offering favorable cosmic influences. Significant numbers in your journey include 7, 16, 25, 34, 43, 52, 61, 70, and 79, marking important stages of change.

Notable Individuals Sharing Your Birthday: Celebrate your April 16 birthday alongside noteworthy individuals, including Anatole France, Wilbur Wright, Charles Chaplin, Peter Ustinov, Kingsley Amis, Henry Mancini, Edie Adams, Herbie Mann, Ellen Barkin, and Selena Quintanilla Perez. Each person born on this day contributes to the diverse tapestry of Aries personalities, embodying the unique interplay of Mars and Neptune.

May your creative visions find practical expression, your relationships be harmonious, and your journey be marked by fulfillment and growth. Embrace the balance between imagination and reality, navigating life with resilience and an open heart.

Astrological Profile for Those Born on April 17

Practicality and Inner Security: Born under the Aries sign with Mars and Saturn as your personal ruling planets, your approach to life is grounded in practicality. However, there is a caution against becoming overly preoccupied with issues of security and money. The pursuit of material acquisition may not fully satisfy your need for inner security. It's crucial to shift your focus from what you lack to appreciating and valuing what you already possess. While you may feel limited and occasionally pessimistic about the future, lifting your spirits by recognizing existing blessings can bring a positive shift.

Spirituality and Evolution: Despite moments of overlooking your spiritual side, your being holds spiritual inclinations. Embracing the subtle and essential elements of nature can enhance your receptivity to spiritual insights. Disappointments through interactions with children might serve as catalysts for further development and evolution. This journey encourages a deeper understanding of your role in society.

Career Path and Financial Considerations: The Birthday Horoscope for April 17 suggests that you possess clear insight into your role in society, making you well-suited for the business world. Fields such as law enforcement and science may also be arenas where you can make a significant impact. Financial prosperity is likely, but caution is advised against excessive risk-taking. Taking steps to protect your assets and adopting a stable, planned approach is crucial. Exceptional communication skills and unique ideas may enhance your professional standing.

Energetic Movement and Leadership Traits: Individuals born on April 17 are characterized by an innate sense of movement, often remaining in constant motion. This restlessness should not be misconstrued as a lack of focus but rather as a manifestation of reliability, hard work, and a strong spiritual connection. Your dynamic nature makes you an excellent candidate for leadership roles in various fields, attracting those with similar traits and aspirations.

Maintaining Stability and Comfort: Taking precautions to protect your assets and avoiding unnecessary risks is advised. Stability and comfort should be prioritized in both financial matters and relationships. Your exceptional communication skills may foster unique ideas, but a conservative approach is recommended to ensure long-term stability.

Lucky Elements: Deep blue and black are your lucky colors, symbolizing depth, stability, and protection. Blue sapphire, lapis lazuli, and amethyst serve as your fortunate gems, aligning with energies that enhance your overall well-being. Wednesdays, Fridays, and Saturdays are designated as your lucky days, carrying favorable cosmic influences. Significant numbers marking stages of change in your journey include 8, 17, 26, 35, 44, 53, 62, and 71.

Notable Individuals Sharing Your Birthday: Celebrate your April 17 birthday alongside notable individuals such as J.P. Morgan, Isak Dinesen, Nikita Khrushchev, Thornton Wilder, William Holden, Harry Reasoner, Sean Bean, Liz Phair, Victoria Adams (Victoria Beckham), and Jennifer de Jong. Each person born on this day contributes to the diverse tapestry of Aries personalities, embodying the unique interplay of Mars and Saturn.

May your journey be marked by a balance of practicality, spiritual insight, and financial stability, leading to fulfillment and growth.

Embrace the positive aspects of your dynamic nature, channeling your energy into constructive endeavors and leadership roles.

Astrological Profile for Those Born on April 18

Fearless Assertiveness and Debating Skills: As an Aries born on April 18, your personal ruling planet is Mars, imbuing you with an unyielding spirit and fearlessness in expressing your opinions. Your assertiveness, sometimes delivered quite loudly, sets you apart. While your debating skills can bring you fortune, it's advised to lighten your manner and practice the art of quiet assertion. Tempering the abrasive side of your nature can prevent constant bickering and squabbling.

Potential Areas of Success: Despite the potential for conflict, your debating prowess can lead to success in law, legal disputes, sales, or diplomatic roles. The assertive energy you possess, coupled with great physical power and pride in your bodily strength, can pave the way for achievements in various domains. However, caution is advised, as indications of possible injury, especially to the knees and ankles, are present.

Dynamic and Empowering Traits: Individuals born on April 18 exhibit bravery and empowerment, embodying the Aries spirit of action and vitality. Restlessness prevails when faced with restrictions, and their physical energies are channeled productively. Typically well-groomed, trim, and healthy, their mental well-being thrives on engagement and productivity. Boredom or loneliness can impact their mental state, emphasizing the need for stimulation.

Optimism and Ambition: A sense of optimism about the future permeates the April 18 personality, driven by a recognition of the vastness of the horizon. This optimism aligns with their ambitious nature, making them likely candidates for success in business, politics, invention, or entrepreneurship. Despite their anxious tendencies, their determination and willingness to act overcome hurdles, and their mix of ambition and creativity propels them toward material success.

Love and Fulfillment: April 18 Aries individuals seek love and loyalty for happiness and fulfillment. They may face challenges in navigating disaster situations, but their resilient spirit prevails. Prone to anxiety due to high energy levels, their determination ensures they overcome obstacles. The personality traits of April 18 Aries are a dynamic blend, creating a multifaceted character driven by ambition and a desire for success.

Lucky Elements: Red, maroon, scarlet, and autumn tones are your lucky colors, symbolizing passion, strength, and vibrancy. Red coral and garnet serve as your fortunate gems, enhancing the positive energies surrounding you. Mondays, Tuesdays, and Thursdays are your lucky days, aligning with cosmic influences favoring your endeavors. Significant numbers marking stages of change include 9, 18, 27, 36, 45, 54, 63, and 72.

Notable Individuals Sharing Your Birthday: Celebrate your April 18 birthday alongside notable individuals such as Leopold Stokowski, Little Brother Montgomery, Hayley Mills, James Woods, Conan O'Brien, Maria Bello, and Melissa Joan Hart. Each person born on this day contributes to the vibrant tapestry of Aries personalities, embodying the unique interplay of Mars' influence.

May your assertiveness be a tool for positive impact, and may your dynamic nature lead you to success in various realms, fueled by ambition, creativity, and an unwavering determination to overcome challenges.

Astrological Profile for Those Born on April 19

Stamina and Dynamism: As an Aries born on April 19, the planetary influences of Mars and the Sun contribute to your remarkable stamina and dynamism. Your energy levels often leave others in awe, and the key words defining your birthdate are power and vigor. While this hard-nosed approach can fuel your ambition, it may pose challenges in personal relationships and long-term love affairs. Consider reassessing priorities and adopting a gentler approach with your loved ones.

Separation and Ambition: Individuals born on April 19 may experience separation from family and close friends or face breakups in relationships. The Aries archetype, with its strong masculine energy, aligns with the ambition and drive often seen in billionaires born under this sign. Your cardinal personality and intense mystical feelings drive a thirst for knowledge and general recognition.

Openness and Ambitious Pursuits: Despite a fiery temperament, those born on April 19 possess openness and honesty, enjoying discussions about themselves and their goals. However, this candid nature may pose challenges in forming fulfilling relationships. Ambitious and courageous, individuals with this birthdate pursue success with unwavering determination, often retaining a childlike spirit throughout their lives. Fearless entrepreneurs, they passionately engage in their pursuits, becoming valuable assets appreciated for their resourcefulness.

Lucky Elements: Copper and gold represent your lucky colors, symbolizing richness and warmth. Ruby serves as your fortunate gem, enhancing the positive energies surrounding you. Sundays, Mondays, and Thursdays are your lucky days, aligning with cosmic influences favoring your endeavors. Significant numbers marking stages of change include 1, 10, 19, 28, 37, 46, 55, 64, 73, and 82.

Notable Individuals Sharing Your Birthday: Celebrate your April 19 birthday alongside notable individuals such as Hugh O'Brien, Jayne Mansfield, Ashley Judd, James Franco, Kate Hudson, and Hayden Christensen. Each person born on this day contributes to the diverse tapestry of Aries personalities, embodying the unique interplay of Mars and Sun influences.

Final Thoughts: May your boundless energy fuel not only your ambitious pursuits but also contribute to harmonious and fulfilling relationships. As you navigate the dynamic interplay of planetary influences, embracing a balance between assertiveness and gentleness will enrich your personal connections and enhance your journey toward success.

Astrological Profile for Those Born on April 20

Dilemmas and Compassion: As an Aries born on April 20, your personal ruling planets are Mars and the Moon, giving rise to a life path marked by dilemmas related to balancing work and home or family. Known as "The Helper" in your professional sphere, you exude a loving and caring energy, often extending beyond your immediate family environment. Emotionally sensitive and possessing psychic tendencies, you may encounter moments of paralysis when torn between the desire to act and emotional constraints.

Receptive Aura and Emotional Expression: Your vibrations suggest that your receptive aura may absorb negative energies from those you assist. It's crucial for you to express your feelings openly, avoiding the bottling up of resentments or guilt. Free expression will help you release emotional burdens and maintain a healthier balance.

Strengths and Weaknesses: The characteristics defining your personality center around warmth, kindness, imaginative curiosity, high motivation, and a thorough approach to tasks. However, lunar-influenced sensitivity can lead to domineering behavior, particularly when upset. This weakness may be less pronounced when you are well-rested, emphasizing the importance of self-care.

Passion and Adventure in Relationships: April 20th personalities are passionate, adventurous, and well-suited for romantic relationships. While they appreciate serious commitments, settling down may not be an immediate priority. Attracted to refined and passionate partners, they seek someone dependable while maintaining their individuality and spirit in the relationship.

Creative and Imaginative Nature: Creativity and imagination characterize those born on April 20, with a penchant for enjoying life and adhering to high standards. Stubbornness and a commitment to convictions are notable traits, along with a love for the outdoors, exploration, and the arts. Expect surprises and excitement if you celebrate your birthday on April 20, revealing the secrets of your creative personality.

Lucky Elements: Cream and white, along with green, are your lucky colors, creating an aura of calm and growth. Moonstone or pearl serves as your fortunate gems, enhancing your connection to lunar influences. Mondays, Thursdays, and Sundays bring luck, aligning with cosmic energies conducive to your pursuits. Significant numbers marking stages of change include 2, 11, 20, 29, 38, 47, 56, 65, and 74.

Famous Individuals Sharing Your Birthday: Celebrate your April 20th birthday alongside notable individuals such as Miro, Adolph Hitler, Jessica Lange, Carmen Electra, Joey Lawrence, and Veronica Cartwright. Each person born on this day contributes to the unique tapestry of Aries personalities, sharing the influences of Mars and the Moon on their life paths.

Astrological Profile for Those Born on April 21

Taurus Traits and Planetary Influences:

If you were born on April 21, your star sign is Taurus, and your personal ruling planets are Venus and Jupiter. This combination bestows upon you a lucky and powerful vibration, setting the stage for comfort, success, and a profound appreciation for material wealth and sensuality.

Temperament and Drive for Success:

Individuals born on April 21 exhibit a stable temperament and possess a strong drive for success. While easy to connect with and exuding confidence, they also display stubborn and inflexible tendencies. Understanding these facets of your personality helps navigate your destiny.

Balance and Moderation:

It's essential to strike a balance and not become overly fixated on material aspects of life. Recognize when enough is enough, as inheritances and wealthy partners may come your way. Practicing moderation in all aspects of life is key to maintaining equilibrium.

Health Considerations:

While those born on April 21 enjoy a robust constitution, they may be susceptible to common colds, throat ailments, and ear problems. Despite their generally good health, a tendency to overeat exists, requiring a focus on moderation. Maintaining a healthy lifestyle, including a balanced diet, adequate sleep, and sugar intake awareness, contributes to overall well-being.

Determination and Patience:

Individuals celebrating their April 21 birthday should prepare for challenges and stress. Despite high energy levels, success requires determination and patience. This period signifies a commitment to pursuing goals and an understanding that finding a soulmate takes time.

Lucky Elements:

Lucky colors include yellow, lemon, and sandy shades, creating an aura of positivity. Yellow sapphire, citrine quartz, and golden topaz serve as fortunate gems. Thursdays, Sundays, and Tuesdays align with favorable cosmic energies, while significant numbers marking stages of change are 3, 12, 21, 30, 39, 48, 57, 66, and 75.

Famous Individuals Sharing Your Birthday:

Celebrate your April 21 birthday alongside notable individuals such as Charlotte Bronte, Anthony Quinn, Queen Elizabeth II, Timothy Dalton, James Morrison, Andie MacDowell, and Toby Stephens. Each person born on this day contributes to the unique tapestry of Taurus personalities, sharing the influences of Venus and Jupiter on their life paths.

Astrological Profile for Those Born on April 22

Taurus Traits with Venus and Uranus Influences:
Born on April 22, your star sign is Taurus, and your personal ruling planets are Venus and Uranus. This unique combination infuses you with a vibrant and electric energy, especially in the realm of relationships. Your livewire personality, equivalent to about a million watts, suggests a progressive attitude, original ideas, and a flair for the unusual.

Adventurous Spirit and Passionate Love:

Your adventurous spirit and passion make you a candidate for a long-term relationship. While your journey may have a rocky start, patience will lead to the right person entering your life. This partner will be passionate, loyal, and relentless, matching your intensity and commitment.

Spontaneity, Adventure, and Aggressiveness:

People born on April 22 are characterized by spontaneity, adventurousness, and a touch of aggressiveness. Known for their extravagant spending and occasional mistakes, they thrive in commitment but can be thrown off balance in new situations. They value their independence but are dedicated and loyal friends.

Surprises in Love and Unique Traits:

Love life for those born on April 22 holds many surprises. While there's a deep desire for love, romantic partners may not be the primary attraction. Surprisingly, many find love within their existing relationships. Success in relationships is more likely when the partner is realistic, pragmatic, and understanding, guiding you in the right direction.

Charismatic Ambition and Family Focus:

Charismatic individuals born after April 22 pursue quality over quantity. Despite a reserved nature, their ambitions are unwavering, easily influencing others. They excel as parents and partners, valuing family bonds and building a strong foundation.

Lucky Colors, Gems, Days, and Numbers:

Electric blue, electric white, and multi-colors are your lucky colors, while Hessonite garnet and agate are your fortunate gems. Sundays and Tuesdays bring positive energy, and the numbers 4, 13, 22, 31, 40, 49, 58, 67, and 76 mark significant stages of change.

Famous Individuals Sharing Your Birthday:

Celebrate your April 22 birthday alongside renowned figures such as Immanuel Kant, Nikolay Lenin, Yehudi Menuhin, Hal March, Glen Campbell, Jack Nicholson, Bettie Page, Sabine Appelmans, and Ambra Angiolini. Each of these individuals contributes to the unique tapestry of personalities shaped by the influences of Venus and Uranus.

Astrological Profile for Those Born on April 23

Taurus Traits with Venus and Mercury Influences:

Born on April 23, your star sign is Taurus, and your personal ruling planets are Venus and Mercury. Your vibrations are marked by refined and artistic qualities, granting you the power of speech, poetry, and effective communication. The speed of your thought is remarkable, leading to quick and generally accurate decisions.

Natural Business Skills and Flexibility:

Endowed with natural business skills, you are drawn to pursuits aligned with Mercury's influence. To enhance your opportunities, consider being more flexible with your opinions and ideas, adapting to the changing times. This openness can lead to broader horizons and increased success.

Amalgamation of Energies and Practicality:

Individuals born on April 23 embody an amalgamation of energies. While they may sometimes feel confused and disconnected, they possess an innate sense of practicality, love, and faith. This unique blend draws them to like-minded individuals who share similar traits.

Lucky Color, Gems, Days, and Numbers:

Green is your lucky color, symbolizing growth and harmony. Emerald, Aquamarine, or Jade are fortunate gems associated with your birth. Wednesdays, Fridays, and Saturdays bring positive energies, and the numbers 5, 14, 23, 32, 41, 50, 59, 68, and 77 mark significant stages of change.

Famous Individuals Sharing Your Birthday:

Celebrate your April 23 birthday alongside notable figures such as William Shakespeare, James A. Buchanan, Ngaio Marsh, Vladimir Nabokov, Shirley Temple, Judy Davis, Corine Boon, Scott Bairstow, and James King. Each of these personalities contributes to the diverse tapestry shaped by the influences of Venus and Mercury.

Embarking on the Venusian Odyssey of April 24 Explorers:

Set sail, dear April 24 cosmic voyagers, under the exquisite guidance of Venus, your celestial captain ruling both the month and the day of your birth. Picture your celestial ship adorned with the essence of love and beauty, as Venus casts its enchanting glow upon your journey.

Harmony in the Cosmic Domestic Sphere:

Imbued with a natural sense of balance, you channel your energy into the realms of family and domesticity. The harmonious vibrations of your celestial abode are of paramount importance, and any disruption sends ripples through your cosmic equilibrium. Perhaps, the cosmic call even draws you to establish your workplace within the comforting embrace of your home.

Venusian Influence on Work and Relationships:

In the cosmic tapestry of your life, work issues may weave a unique pattern involving female co-workers. Venus, the planet of love, extends its influence beyond personal relationships, casting a gentle glow on your professional collaborations. As you navigate the cosmic currents of your career, the harmonious flow of energies is essential for your flourishing.

The Multifaceted Tapestry of April 24 Personalities:

Dive into the depths of your personality, where energy, generosity, and compassion interweave. Your cosmic persona shines with good looks and a delightful sense of humor. A skilled communicator and manager, you wield patience and pragmatism as cosmic tools. Yet, the occasional shadows of indecisiveness and moodiness add intricate layers to your celestial tapestry.

Cosmic Creativity and Resourcefulness:

April 24-born individuals are blessed with imaginative creativity, clever resourcefulness, and a strong willpower that propels them towards their goals. Their ability to tap into community resources enhances their cosmic journey, making them adept navigators of the unknown.

Navigating the Celestial Seas with Care:

As you sail through the cosmic seas, remember to keep your boundaries and temper in check. The delicate dance of white and cream, rose and pink hues adorns your celestial vessel, while diamond, white sapphire, or quartz crystal gems glisten like stars in your cosmic toolkit.

Celestial Companions on Your Odyssey: Famous Figures Aboard:

Imagine sharing this cosmic odyssey with luminaries such as Anthony Trollope, Robert P. Warren, Shirley Maclaine, Barbra Streisand, Gemi Taylor, and Kimberley Cooper. Each figure contributes to the celestial mosaic, creating a rich and vibrant cosmic tapestry.

Lucky Colors and Gems Illuminate Your Path:

In the radiant glow of your Venusian journey, embrace the lucky colors that adorn your cosmic vessel — white and cream, rose and pink hues. Let these hues infuse your odyssey with harmony and balance.

As you navigate the celestial seas, let the sparkle of diamond, white sapphire, or quartz crystal gems be your guiding stars. These cosmic treasures illuminate your path, adding brilliance to your cosmic toolkit.

So, with Venus as your guiding star, adorned in lucky colors and gems, embark on this cosmic journey, embracing the harmonious energies that surround you!

April 25: Taurus Tapestry of Idealism and Generosity

For those celebrating their birthday on April 25, the cosmic ballet places you under the enchanting sign of Taurus, where the graceful dance of Venus and Neptune guides your celestial journey. This divine partnership weaves a tapestry of idealism and generosity, creating a unique essence that shapes your vibrant persona. Let's delve into the cosmic revelations that define your astrological identity.

Taurus Radiance with Venus and Neptune

In the celestial symphony of Taurus, Venus, the planet of love and beauty, entwines with Neptune, the dreamweaver. This union bestows upon you a perfect balance of aesthetic appreciation and spiritual yearning. Your essence radiates elegance and altruism, casting an enchanting aura that captivates those around you.

Idealistic Temptations and Psychic Gifts: Balancing Acts

Your journey is adorned with an idealistic temperament, fueled by a perpetual quest for spiritual principles. However, this generous nature may become a double-edged sword, as family and friends might take advantage of your giving heart. Your innate psychic and intuitive abilities serve as a guiding light—use them to scrutinize the intentions of others and navigate potential pitfalls.

Passionate Leadership and Ambitious Ventures: The Taurus Quest

April 25 births mark the initiation of a journey fueled by ambition and a pursuit of perfection in every endeavor. Your passion not only propels your work forward but also pushes you to embrace calculated risks. While these ventures may lead to unforeseen outcomes, your visionary spirit remains associated with family, love, and financial prosperity. Maintain realistic expectations as you embark on your pursuits.

Openness, Directness, and Perseverance: Traits Unveiled

Individuals born on April 25 exhibit traits of openness, directness, and unwavering perseverance. Despite occasional impatience and restlessness, their sharp intellect positions them as valuable assets in leadership roles. Their sense of responsibility is commendable, aligning with their aptitude for effective leadership.

Driven by Ambition: The Taurus Journey

Driven by ambition, April 25th individuals fearlessly tread the extra mile to achieve their goals. Their readiness to assume leadership positions is complemented by a keen awareness of the associated responsibilities and consequences. Love unfolds early and profoundly for them, often resulting in early marriages once they feel ready to embark on such significant life milestones.

Astrological Nuggets for April 25 Birthdays:

• **Lucky Colors:** Embrace the allure of darker green shades.

• **Lucky Gems:** Turquoise, cats eye chrysoberyl, tigers eye bring good fortune.

• **Fortunate Days:** Bask in the cosmic energy on Mondays and Thursdays.

• **Numbers for Success:** Navigate through life's changes with confidence, recognizing the significance of 7, 16, 25, 34, 43, 52, 61, 70, 79.

Notable Individuals Sharing Your Birthday: Celebrate your April 25th birthday alongside the likes of Ella Fitzgerald, Johnny Shines, Albert King, Al Pacino, Hank Azaria, Jason Wiles, and Renee

Zellweger. Each of these figures contributes to the rich tapestry of individuals born on this remarkable date, sharing in the unique qualities and cosmic influences that shape their journeys.

Embrace your cosmic identity, and may each passing year bring new adventures, personal growth, and an abundance of joy on your April 25th journey through life.

Astrological Insight for April 26 Born Individuals

If your birthday falls on April 26, under the enduring sign of Taurus, guided by the celestial forces of Venus and Saturn, you embody a unique blend of high principles, practicality, and visionary pursuits. Let's unravel the cosmic revelations that shape your distinct astrological profile.

Noble Principles and Benevolent Actions

Your essence resonates with high principles, reflecting a commitment to doing what's right for others. While you may not explicitly label yourself as religious, your life is a testament to ethical living, creating a positive ripple effect on your destiny. Your approach is steeped in benevolence, and this moral compass guides your interactions and choices.

Structured Thinking with a Cautionary Note

The architecture of your thoughts is built upon pillars of structure, order, and discipline. A potential challenge lies in an inclination to plan excessively. While strategic thinking is an asset, cultivating flexibility in your dreams and relationships can open doors to unforeseen opportunities and enrich your life journey.

Practical Visionaries of April 26

As a Taurus born on April 26, you embody a balance of practicality and visionary spirit. A strong desire for preservation may coexist with a penchant for the arts. This juxtaposition encourages you to navigate life with a blend of pragmatism and creativity. Embrace this duality to carve a unique path tailored to your passions and aspirations.

Dedicated Work Ethic and Considerate Communication

Dedication marks your professional endeavors, and your colleagues recognize you as a hardworking and reliable team member. While your work ethic is commendable, your ability to listen and avoid insensitivity sets you apart. Being an excellent listener, balance it by refining your communication style, steering clear of cynicism or rudeness.

The Taurus Element: Determination and Comfort

As a Taurus, determination and stubbornness define your character. You value comfort in all aspects of life but refuse to compromise on attaining it. Challenges only fuel your willpower and unwavering determination. Your resilience in the face of adversity can serve as an inspiration to fellow Tauruses, showcasing the strength inherent in your astrological sign.

Love, Romance, and Decision-Making Acumen

Taurus, the sign of love and romance, finds a unique expression in your decision-making skills. While you're discerning about romantic partners, your natural ability to connect shines through. In matters of love, your sign's compatibility and decision-making prowess guide you towards fulfilling connections. Be mindful of the company you keep, as your circle may shape your romantic experiences.

Astrological Nuggets for April 26 Birthdays:

- **Lucky Colors:** Deep blue and black enhance your positive energy.
- **Lucky Gems:** Blue sapphire, lapis lazuli, and amethyst attract good fortune.
- **Fortunate Days:** Wednesday, Friday, and Saturday bring cosmic alignment.
- **Numbers for Success:** Navigate life's changes with confidence using 8, 17, 26, 35, 44, 53, 62, 71.

Notable Individuals Sharing Your Birthday: Celebrate your April 26th birthday alongside esteemed figures like Marcus Aurelius, Oliver Cromwell, Carol Burnett, Jet Li, and Jordana Brewster. Each contributes to the rich tapestry of individuals born on this remarkable date, sharing in the unique qualities and cosmic influences that shape their journeys.

Embrace your cosmic identity, and may each passing year bring new adventures, personal growth, and an abundance of joy on your April 26th journey through life.

Astrological Insight for April 27 Born Individuals

If your birthday falls on April 27, under the steadfast sign of Taurus, governed by the cosmic dance of Venus and Mars, you radiate a passionate energy that fuels both your professional pursuits and personal connections. Let's delve deeper into the celestial revelations that shape your unique astrological profile.

Passionate Flames and Unyielding Determination

A fiery passion courses through your soul, refusing to be extinguished. In both work and play, you embrace an "all or nothing at all" approach, pushing yourself with unwavering determination. However, be mindful of the intensity you bring into your relationships; striking a balance can prevent unintentional burns. Remember, moderation can be the key to sustained flames.

Navigating Relationships and Business

Your zeal for partnerships can be intense, but it's essential not to become overly obsessed. Maintaining a balance between personal and professional realms is crucial. A piece of cosmic advice encourages you to be mindful of intertwining business and relationships. Additionally, the stars hint at the potential for a marriage with someone from a foreign land, adding a touch of celestial diversity to your life.

Practicality and Stability in Life

Individuals born on April 27 embody a practical approach to life, finding solace in the benefits of stability and order. Confidence accompanies their measured approach to love, as they meticulously weigh all options before committing. Physical well-being is highlighted, with emphasis on caring for the sensitive neck and throat areas. Seeking professional advice for health matters ensures a steady and robust life journey.

Intuition and Decision-Making Prowess

April 27 births are graced with a high level of intuition, lending an air of tact to their interactions. While their intuitive powers are potent, aligning them with effective decision-making, it's crucial to nurture this innate gift. Adequate sleep becomes a celestial prescription, enhancing their intuitive faculties and overall well-being.

Skillful Individuals with Social Grace

Individuals born on April 27 harbor grand aspirations, often wrestling with the challenge of connecting their diverse skills. Adaptability marks their journey, as they might switch between skills learned over the years. While they may grapple with sticking to a schedule, their steady personality shines in social environments. Exceptional social skills and a keen mind make them valuable friends, creating harmonious connections in safe spaces.

Astrological Nuggets for April 27 Birthdays:

• **Lucky Colors:** Red, maroon, scarlet, and autumn tones infuse positive energy.

• **Lucky Gems:** Red coral and garnet enhance good fortune.

• **Fortunate Days:** Monday, Tuesday, and Thursday align with cosmic energy.

• **Numbers for Success:** Navigate life's changes confidently with 9, 18, 27, 36, 45, 54, 63, 72.

Notable Individuals Sharing Your Birthday: Celebrate your April 27th birthday alongside influential figures like Herbert Spencer, Ulysses S. Grant, Sheena Easton, and Michael Mahonen. Each contributes to the rich tapestry of individuals born on this remarkable date, sharing in the unique qualities and cosmic influences that shape their journeys.

Embrace your cosmic identity, and may each passing year bring new adventures, personal growth, and an abundance of joy on your April 27th journey through life.

Astrological Insight for April 28 Born Individuals

If your birthday falls on April 28, under the steadfast sign of Taurus, influenced by the celestial dance of Venus and the Sun, your astrological profile unveils a person deeply rooted in a quest for identity, stability, and success. Let's unravel the cosmic tapestry that shapes your unique characteristics and journey.

Desire for Identity and Safe Havens

A profound desire for a safe haven and a strong connection to your roots characterize your nature. You seek a deep understanding of your identity and historical past, finding confidence in knowing where you come from. This knowledge becomes a beacon guiding your path, instilling the assurance needed to navigate the complexities of life.

Earthly Talents and Career Pathways

Blessed with a talent for handling property, land, and earthly matters, you may find joy in activities like gardening. Consider career paths in real estate, mining, or development, where your innate skills can flourish. Your leadership qualities and unwavering determination propel you towards achievements, with a resolute attitude of never saying "can't."

Stability, Kindness, and Loyalty

April 28th birthdays paint a picture of stability, kindness, and loyalty. Creativity flows through your veins, enhancing your awareness and making you a romantic soul. While responsibility and impulsiveness may coexist within you, be cautious not to mistake these traits for weakness. Managing pressure may present challenges, but your inherent fighting spirit ensures you overcome hurdles.

Love and Relationships

In matters of the heart, you seek a long-lasting, loving relationship marked by affection and harmony. Averse to conflict and drama, you yearn for a partner who makes you feel cherished and special. While you savor a romantic life, cultivating self-confidence and taking time for personal growth remain essential. Your birthday heralds an opportunity for emotional balance and healing from past traumas.

Outgoing Nature and Social Charms

The April 28 Birthday Horoscope highlights your outgoing and social nature. Guard against stubbornness, allowing flexibility to enrich your interactions. The benefits of your birthday extend beyond personal growth, contributing to the positive energies you bring to your social circles.

Astrological Nuggets for April 28 Birthdays:

• **Lucky Colors:** Copper and gold infuse positive energies into your life.

• **Lucky Gem:** Ruby enhances good fortune.

• **Fortunate Days:** Sunday, Monday, and Thursday align with cosmic energies.

• **Numbers for Success:** Navigate through life's changes with confidence, recognizing the significance of 1, 10, 19, 28, 37, 46, 55, 64, 73, and 82.

Notable Individuals Sharing Your Birthday: Celebrate your April 28th birthday alongside influential figures like James Monroe, Lionel Barrymore, Jay Leno, Jessica Alba, and others. Each contributes to the rich tapestry of individuals born on this remarkable date, sharing in the unique qualities and cosmic influences that shape their journeys.

Embrace your cosmic identity, and may each passing year bring new adventures, personal growth, and an abundance of joy on your April 28th journey through life.

Astrological Insight for April 29 Born Individuals

If your birthday falls on April 29, under the steadfast sign of Taurus, guided by the cosmic dance of Venus and the Moon, your astrological profile unveils a complex yet fascinating personality. Let's delve into the celestial influences shaping your restless spirit, insatiable quest for knowledge, and the harmonious energy you bring to relationships.

Restless Soul Seeking Security

A dichotomy defines your essence—desiring security above all yet compelled to keep moving. Your restlessness extends beyond physical travels; it encompasses journeys of the mind and spirit. Even in moments of settlement, your thoughts dance like the wind. Embrace the perpetual learning curve, for you are the eternal student, constantly seeking knowledge. However, heed the ancient wisdom: "knowledge is bondage." Recognize when to say "enough is enough" and find equilibrium.

Lucky and Farsighted Nature

Born on April 29, you carry the gifts of luck and foresight. Cautious and careful, you navigate through life with a prudent mindset—trusting, yet verifying. While your travels may span the world, your understanding of others and your ability to present your best self contribute to the harmonious relationships you cultivate. Your sociability, understanding of needs, and desire for stability make you a cherished friend and family member.

Peaceful, Purposeful, and Easy-Going

Individuals born on April 29 embody qualities of peace, purpose, and easy-going nature. Averse to instability, you seek the comfort of a stable environment. Despite a penchant for immaturity in love, your focus remains on avoiding uncertainty and risky situations. Throat conditions, colds, and indigestion may be occasional challenges, yet your well-being thrives in the embrace of friends and family.

Charm, Humor, and Positive Outlook

The charm, humor, and positive outlook you exude inspire those around you. While competitiveness drives you, maintain caution to avoid accidents stemming from overzealous efforts. Cultivate careful planning and a holistic perspective, never losing sight of the bigger picture. Enjoy the journey, relishing every moment.

Astrological Nuggets for April 29 Birthdays:

• **Lucky Colors:** Cream, white, and green infuse positivity into your life.

• **Lucky Gems:** Moonstone or pearl enhance your innate strengths.

• **Fortunate Days:** Monday, Thursday, and Sunday align with cosmic energies.

• **Numbers for Success:** Navigate life's changes with confidence, recognizing the significance of 2, 11, 20, 29, 38, 47, 56, 65, and 74.

Notable Individuals Sharing Your Birthday: Celebrate your April 29th birthday alongside influential figures like Duke Ellington, Jerry Seinfeld, Michelle Pfeiffer, Uma Thurman, and others. Each contributes to the rich tapestry of individuals born on this remarkable date, sharing in the unique qualities and cosmic influences that shape their journeys.

Embrace your cosmic identity, and may each passing year bring new adventures, personal growth, and an abundance of joy on your April 29th journey through life.

Astrological Insights for April 30 Born Individuals

If your birthday falls on April 30, under the enduring sign of Taurus, guided by the celestial dance of Venus and Jupiter, your astrological profile unveils a unique blend of luck, magnanimity, and a penchant for pleasure. Let's explore the cosmic influences shaping your character, relationships, and the exciting journey that lies ahead.

Born Lucky with Jupiter and Venus Vibrations

Consider yourself born under a fortunate star. The harmonious vibrations of Jupiter and Venus bestow upon you a special path. However, take heed, for luck should not be taken for granted. While you may be blessed with financial assistance or resources, the key lies in valuing these gifts and taking initiative in your life's pursuits.

Big Plans, Magnanimous Heart, and Soft Nature

April 30 birthdays are marked by individuals with grand aspirations and a heart generous in spirit. Yet, there's a risk of not easily holding onto achievements due to a soft nature and a love for pleasure and luxury. Impatience and overprotectiveness may surface, adding layers to your dynamic personality. Your ability to temper stubbornness through experiences is a noteworthy trait.

Passionate, Independent, and Stubborn Lovers

In matters of love, you are a loyal and passionate partner. However, a tendency to study potential partners before committing can make relationships initially platonic. Independence and homeliness coexist within you, but togetherness might pose a challenge. Balancing your adventurous spirit with a desire for a partner to share feelings and fun becomes a significant aspect of your romantic journey.

Astrological Nuggets for April 30 Birthdays:

• **Lucky Colors:** Embrace the vibrancy of yellow, lemon, and sandy shades.

• **Lucky Gems:** Adorn yourself with the brilliance of yellow sapphire, citrine quartz, and golden topaz.

• **Fortunate Days:** Thursday, Sunday, and Tuesday align with cosmic energies.

• **Numbers for Success:** Navigate through life's changes with confidence by recognizing the significance of 3, 12, 21, 30, 39, 48, 57, 66, and 75.

Notable Individuals Sharing Your Birthday: Celebrate your April 30th birthday alongside influential figures like Eve Arden, Cloris Leachman, Perry King, and Kirsten Dunst. Each contributes to the rich tapestry of individuals born on this remarkable date, sharing in the unique qualities and cosmic influences that shape their journeys.

Embrace your cosmic identity, and may each passing year bring new adventures, personal growth, and an abundance of joy on your April 30th journey through life.

Examples of famous individuals born under each element.

Certainly! Let's explore famous individuals born under each astrological element in 'The Secret Language of Birthdays April Profiles.' These examples showcase the diverse personalities and achievements associated with the unique energies of fire, earth, air, and water.

Fire Signs:

1. **Aries (March 21 - April 19):**

   • Example: Lady Gaga

   • Contribution: Lady Gaga, born on March 28, is known for her passionate performances, dynamic creativity, and fearless approach to the entertainment industry.

2. **Leo (July 23 - August 22):**

   • Example: Barack Obama

   • Contribution: Barack Obama, born on August 4, exhibits the leadership and charisma characteristic of Leos. He served as the 44th President of the United States.

3. **Sagittarius (November 22 - December 21):**

• Example: Taylor Swift

• Contribution: Taylor Swift, born on December 13, is a Sagittarius known for her adventurous spirit, optimistic outlook, and prolific career in music.

Earth Signs:
1. **Taurus (April 20 - May 20):**

• Example: Adele

• Contribution: Adele, born on May 5, embodies the stability and practicality of Taurus. Her soulful music and grounded demeanor have made her a global sensation.

2. **Virgo (August 23 - September 22):**

• Example: Beyoncé

• Contribution: Beyoncé, born on September 4, is a Virgo known for her precision, hard work, and meticulous approach to her craft in the music and entertainment industry.

3. **Capricorn (December 22 - January 19):**

• Example: Michelle Obama

• Contribution: Michelle Obama, born on January 17, exemplifies the disciplined and responsible nature of Capricorns. She served as the First Lady of the United States.

Air Signs:

1. **Gemini (May 21 - June 20):**

• Example: Angelina Jolie

• Contribution: Angelina Jolie, born on June 4, showcases the adaptability and intellectual curiosity of Geminis. She is renowned for her acting, directing, and humanitarian work.

2. **Libra (September 23 - October 22):**

• Example: Will Smith

• Contribution: Will Smith, born on September 25, embodies the harmonious and sociable traits of Libras. His success spans acting, music, and philanthropy.

3. **Aquarius (January 20 - February 18):**

• Example: Oprah Winfrey

• Contribution: Oprah Winfrey, born on January 29, is an Aquarius known for her innovative thinking, humanitarian efforts, and impactful career in media.

Water Signs:
1. **Cancer (June 21 - July 22):**

• Example: Princess Diana

• Contribution: Princess Diana, born on July 1, epitomized the nurturing and empathetic qualities of Cancer. Her humanitarian work and compassion left a lasting impact.

2. **Scorpio (October 23 - November 21):**

- Example: Leonardo DiCaprio

- Contribution: Leonardo DiCaprio, born on November 11, reflects the intensity and transformative nature of Scorpios. His acting career and environmental activism demonstrate his passion.

3. Pisces (February 19 - March 20):

- Example: Rihanna

- Contribution: Rihanna, born on February 20, embodies the creative and compassionate spirit of Pisces. Her success in music, fashion, and philanthropy showcases her diverse talents.

In 'The Secret Language of Birthdays April Profiles,' we explore how these famous individuals' birthdates and associated elements contribute to their unique personalities and achievements. Get ready to discover the cosmic threads that weave through the lives of these iconic figures!

Iconic figures born on different days.

Certainly! Let's highlight iconic figures born on different days across the calendar in 'The Secret Language of Birthdays April Profiles.' These individuals, each with their unique contributions, have left a lasting impact on various fields.

1. **January 8: Elvis Presley (Capricorn):**

• Contribution: Known as the "King of Rock and Roll," Elvis Presley, born on January 8, revolutionized the music industry with his charismatic performances and iconic voice.

2. **February 12: Abraham Lincoln (Aquarius):**

• Contribution: Abraham Lincoln, born on February 12, was the 16th President of the United States and played a pivotal role in the abolition of slavery during the Civil War.

3. **March 14: Albert Einstein (Pisces):**

• Contribution: Albert Einstein, born on March 14, was a theoretical physicist whose groundbreaking work revolutionized our understanding of space, time, and energy with the theory of relativity.

4. **April 23: William Shakespeare (Taurus):**

• Contribution: William Shakespeare, born on April 23, is widely regarded as one of the greatest playwrights and poets in history, leaving an indelible mark on literature with his timeless works.

5. May 29: John F. Kennedy (Gemini):

• Contribution: John F. Kennedy, born on May 29, was the 35th President of the United States. His leadership during the Cuban Missile Crisis and commitment to civil rights are notable aspects of his legacy.

6. June 18: Paul McCartney (Gemini):

• Contribution: Paul McCartney, born on June 18, is a legendary musician and songwriter, co-founding The Beatles and contributing to numerous iconic songs in the history of music.

7. July 20: Nikola Tesla (Cancer):

• Contribution: Nikola Tesla, born on July 20, was an inventor and engineer known for his contributions to the development of alternating current (AC) electrical systems and numerous innovations in technology.

8. August 29: Ingrid Bergman (Virgo):

• Contribution: Ingrid Bergman, born on August 29, was a highly acclaimed actress, known for her performances in classic films like "Casablanca" and "Notorious."

9. September 15: Agatha Christie (Virgo):

• Contribution: Agatha Christie, born on September 15, was a renowned mystery novelist, creating iconic characters like Hercule Poirot and Miss Marple, and becoming one of the best-selling authors in history.

10. October 28: Bill Gates (Scorpio):

• Contribution: Bill Gates, born on October 28, co-founded Microsoft and played a pivotal role in the personal computer revolution, becoming a leading figure in the technology industry.

11. November 30: Winston Churchill (Sagittarius):

• Contribution: Winston Churchill, born on November 30, was a statesman and Prime Minister of the United Kingdom, leading the country through the challenges of World War II.

12. December 25: Sir Isaac Newton (Capricorn):

• Contribution: Sir Isaac Newton, born on December 25 (Julian calendar; January 4, 1643, in the Gregorian calendar), was a mathematician and physicist whose laws of motion and universal gravitation revolutionized physics.

These iconic figures born on different days showcase the diversity of talent and accomplishments across various fields. In 'The Secret Language of Birthdays April Profiles,' we explore how the cosmic influences associated with these birthdates contribute to the richness of their personalities and legacies.

Explore their achievements and how their birthdate might have influenced their paths.

Certainly! Let's explore the achievements of iconic figures born on different days in 'The Secret Language of Birthdays April Profiles' and consider how their birthdates might have influenced their paths.

1. **Elvis Presley (Born January 8, Capricorn):**

• **Achievements:** Elvis Presley, the "King of Rock and Roll," revolutionized music with his charismatic performances and chart-topping hits. He became a cultural icon and is one of the best-selling solo artists in the history of recorded music.

• **Influence of Birthdate:** As a Capricorn, Elvis's determination, discipline, and ambition likely played a role in his sustained success. Capricorns are known for their work ethic and ability to achieve their goals through perseverance.

2. **Abraham Lincoln (Born February 12, Aquarius):**

• **Achievements:** Abraham Lincoln served as the 16th President of the United States and played a pivotal role in the abolition of slavery during the Civil War. His leadership and eloquence are remembered in history.

• **Influence of Birthdate:** Aquarians are often associated with progressive thinking and a commitment to social justice. Lincoln's humanitarian ideals and forward-thinking approach align with the qualities often attributed to Aquarius.

3. **Albert Einstein (Born March 14, Pisces):**

• **Achievements:** Albert Einstein, a theoretical physicist, formulated the theory of relativity, transforming our understanding of space, time, and energy. His contributions to science earned him the Nobel Prize in Physics.

- **Influence of Birthdate:** Pisceans are known for their imaginative and creative minds. Einstein's ability to envision complex concepts and think outside the box aligns with the intuitive and visionary nature often associated with Pisces.

4. William Shakespeare (Born April 23, Taurus):

- **Achievements:** William Shakespeare is one of the most celebrated playwrights and poets in history. His timeless works, including "Romeo and Juliet" and "Hamlet," continue to influence literature and the arts.

- **Influence of Birthdate:** Taurus individuals are often associated with a love for the arts and a grounded approach to creativity. Shakespeare's enduring impact and ability to capture the human experience resonate with the practical and artistic nature of Taurus.

5. John F. Kennedy (Born May 29, Gemini):

- **Achievements:** John F. Kennedy served as the 35th President of the United States, emphasizing civil rights, space exploration, and international diplomacy. His charisma and leadership left a lasting legacy.

- **Influence of Birthdate:** Geminis are known for their adaptability, communication skills, and intellectual curiosity. Kennedy's ability to connect with people and navigate complex issues aligns with the qualities often associated with Gemini.

6. Paul McCartney (Born June 18, Gemini):

- **Achievements:** Paul McCartney is a legendary musician, singer, and songwriter, known for co-founding The Beatles and contributing to countless hits. His musical influence spans decades.

- **Influence of Birthdate:** Gemini's versatility, communicative skills, and love for variety resonate with McCartney's ability to create diverse and timeless music. The adaptability of Geminis is reflected in his musical exploration.

7. Nikola Tesla (Born July 20, Cancer):

- **Achievements:** Nikola Tesla was an inventor and engineer who made significant contributions to the development of alternating current (AC) electrical systems. His innovations paved the way for modern power systems.

- **Influence of Birthdate:** Cancers are often associated with intuition and emotional depth. Tesla's imaginative and intuitive approach to inventions aligns with the qualities often attributed to Cancer.

8. Ingrid Bergman (Born August 29, Virgo):

- **Achievements:** Ingrid Bergman was a highly acclaimed actress, known for her performances in classic films like "Casablanca" and "Notorious." She received numerous awards for her contributions to cinema.

- **Influence of Birthdate:** Virgos are known for their attention to detail and practicality. Bergman's precision in portraying characters and her dedication to her craft align with the meticulous nature often associated with Virgo.

9. Agatha Christie (Born September 15, Virgo):

• **Achievements:** Agatha Christie was a prolific mystery novelist, creating iconic characters like Hercule Poirot and Miss Marple. She became one of the best-selling authors in history.

• **Influence of Birthdate:** Virgos are often associated with analytical thinking. Christie's ability to craft intricate mysteries and intricate plots reflects the analytical and detail-oriented nature of Virgo.

10. Bill Gates (Born October 28, Scorpio):

• **Achievements:** Bill Gates co-founded Microsoft and played a pivotal role in the personal computer revolution. He became a leading figure in the technology industry and a prominent philanthropist.

• **Influence of Birthdate:** Scorpios are often associated with determination and a transformative approach. Gates' drive for success, transformative influence in technology, and commitment to philanthropy align with Scorpio traits

How birthday profiles impact compatibility in relationships.

Let's explore how birthday profiles impact compatibility in relationships in 'The Secret Language of Birthdays April Profiles.' Understanding the astrological and numerological aspects of individuals can offer insights into their personalities, preferences, and potential dynamics when forming connections with others.

1. **Zodiac Signs and Compatibility:**

• **Understanding Sun Signs:** Knowing each person's sun sign provides a glimpse into their fundamental traits and characteristics. Some signs naturally harmonize, while others may present challenges.

• **Compatibility Factors:** Elements (Fire, Earth, Air, Water) play a role; for instance, Fire signs often align well with Air signs, and Earth signs may find compatibility with Water signs.

2. **Numerology and Relationship Dynamics:**

• **Life Path Numbers:** The life path number, derived from the birthdate, reveals the individual's life purpose. Compatibility can be influenced by the compatibility of life path numbers between partners.

• **Expression Numbers:** Expression numbers reflect how individuals express themselves. Aligning or complementing expression numbers may contribute to a more harmonious relationship.

3. Sun-Moon Combinations:

• **Sun and Moon Signs:** Examining both sun and moon signs provides a more comprehensive view of an individual's emotional and core characteristics.

• **Balancing Energies:** Compatibility can be enhanced when partners' sun and moon signs complement each other, creating a balance of energies in the relationship.

4. Elemental Harmony:

• **Balancing Elements:** A mix of elements in a relationship can contribute to balance. For example, a Fire sign may bring enthusiasm, while an Earth sign provides stability.

• **Understanding Differences:** Recognizing elemental differences can help navigate potential challenges. Water signs, for instance, may bring emotional depth, which may need understanding from more pragmatic Earth signs.

5. Communication Styles:

• **Mercury Sign Influence:** Mercury, the planet of communication, plays a role in how individuals express themselves verbally and intellectually.

- **Harmonizing Communication:** Compatible Mercury signs may contribute to effective communication, fostering understanding and reducing misunderstandings.

6. Personal Growth and Challenges:

- **Numerology Insights:** Numerology can offer insights into areas of personal growth and potential challenges for each individual.

- **Supportive Relationships:** Understanding and supporting each other's journey for personal growth contributes to a healthy and evolving relationship.

7. Timing and Synchronicity:

- **Consideration of Timing:** The timing of birthdays and life events can influence compatibility. Certain life path numbers or astrological aspects may align more favorably during specific periods.

- **Synchronicity:** Partners experiencing significant life events or transitions simultaneously may find a deeper connection through shared experiences.

In 'The Secret Language of Birthdays April Profiles,' we explore how these elements come together to shape the compatibility between individuals. While astrological and numerological insights provide valuable information, it's essential to approach relationships with open communication, mutual respect, and a willingness to understand and appreciate each other's unique qualities. Compatibility is a complex interplay of various factors, and the exploration of birthday profiles adds a colorful layer to the tapestry of relationships.

potential challenges and strengths based on birthdates

Certainly! Let's delve into potential challenges and strengths based on birthdates in 'The Secret Language of Birthdays April Profiles.' While these insights are generalizations and may not apply to every individual, they offer a broad overview of tendencies associated with specific birthdates.

1. **January 8 (Capricorn):**

   - **Strengths:**
   - Determination and Ambition
   - Practical and Grounded Approach
   - Leadership Skills
   - **Challenges:**
   - Tendency to be Overly Serious
   - Struggle with Expressing Emotions
   - Fear of Failure

2. **February 12 (Aquarius):**

   - **Strengths:**
   - Forward-Thinking and Innovative
   - Humanitarian Values
   - Intellectual Curiosity

- **Challenges:**
- Tendency to Be Aloof
- Difficulty with Emotional Expression
- Resistance to Conformity

3. March 14 (Pisces):

- **Strengths:**
- Imaginative and Creative
- Compassionate and Empathetic
- Intuitive and Spiritual
- **Challenges:**
- Prone to Escapism
- Sensitivity to Criticism
- Boundary Issues

4. April 23 (Taurus):

- **Strengths:**
- Practical and Reliable
- Strong Work Ethic
- Appreciation for Beauty
- **Challenges:**
- Stubbornness
- Resistance to Change
- Materialistic Tendencies

5. May 29 (Gemini):

- **Strengths:**
- Versatile and Adaptable
- Excellent Communication Skills
- Curious and Intellectually Driven

- **Challenges:**
- Restlessness
- Difficulty with Commitment
- Prone to Scatter Focus

6. **June 18 (Gemini):**

- **Strengths:**
- Artistic and Musical Talents
- Charming and Social
- Versatility in Creative Expression
- **Challenges:**
- Dual Nature Leading to Indecision
- Prone to Superficiality
- Restlessness in Relationships

7. **July 20 (Cancer):**

- **Strengths:**
- Nurturing and Protective
- Intuitive and Emotionally Intelligent
- Strong Family Bonds
- **Challenges:**
- Vulnerability to Mood Swings
- Tendency to Cling to the Past
- Difficulty Letting Go

8. **August 29 (Virgo):**

- **Strengths:**
- Detail-Oriented and Analytical
- Practical Problem-Solving Skills
- Service-Oriented and Helpful

- **Challenges:**
- Perfectionism
- Overcritical of Self and Others
- Difficulty Delegating

9. **September 15 (Virgo):**

- **Strengths:**
- Sharp Analytical Skills
- Meticulous Planning and Organization
- Creative Problem-Solving
- **Challenges:**
- Tendency to Worry Excessively
- Self-Doubt
- Struggle with Relaxation

10. **October 28 (Scorpio):**

- **Strengths:**
- Intense and Passionate
- Determined and Resilient
- Strong Intuition
- **Challenges:**
- Tendency to Be Secretive
- Fear of Vulnerability
- Prone to Jealousy

11. **November 30 (Sagittarius):**

- **Strengths:**
- Adventurous and Optimistic
- Philosophical and Open-Minded
- Charismatic and Enthusiastic

- **Challenges:**
- Impulsive Decision-Making
- Tendency to Be Restless
- Bluntness in Communication

12. **December 25 (Capricorn):**

- **Strengths:**
- Ambitious and Goal-Oriented
- Disciplined and Responsible
- Practical Problem-Solving Skills
- **Challenges:**
- Struggle with Expressing Emotions
- Overemphasis on Material Success
- Difficulty Delegating

These insights provide a broad overview, and it's crucial to remember that individual personalities are influenced by a combination of factors beyond birthdates. Personal growth and self-awareness can help individuals navigate challenges and leverage their strengths for a more fulfilling life.

Embark on a fascinating journey of self-discovery by unraveling the secrets of your own birthday profile! In 'The Secret Language of Birthdays April Profiles,' the magic lies in understanding the unique blend of astrological and numerological influences that shape your personality, strengths, and potential challenges.

Unlock Your Cosmic Blueprint:

- Dive into the exploration of your sun sign, moon sign, and life path number. These elements offer profound insights into your core traits, emotional nuances, and life's purpose.

Astrological Adventure:

• Discover the celestial dance of the planets at the time of your birth. Your astrological chart is a personalized map that unveils the positions of the stars and their impact on your life.

Numerology Nuggets:

• Decode the vibrations of your birthdate and explore the significance of your life path, expression, and other key numbers. Each number carries a unique energy that shapes your journey.

Celebrate Your Uniqueness:

• Embrace the strengths associated with your birthdate, whether it's the determination of a Capricorn, the creativity of a Pisces, or the adventurous spirit of a Sagittarius. Your individuality is a cosmic masterpiece.

Navigate Challenges with Insight:

• Uncover potential challenges and areas for growth. Awareness is the first step toward overcoming obstacles and turning them into opportunities for personal development.

Build Meaningful Connections:

• Understand how your birthday profile influences your interactions with others. Explore compatibility with friends, family, and potential partners to create more harmonious relationships.

Reflect and Evolve:

• Use your birthday profile as a tool for self-reflection. Consider how your astrological and numerological influences align with your life experiences and personal journey.

Mark Your Cosmic Calendar:

• Celebrate significant astrological events and planetary transits that may impact your life. Tune into the cosmic energies to navigate life's twists and turns with a deeper understanding.

Connect with a Cosmic Community:

• Join others on a similar exploration. Share insights, experiences, and discoveries with a community that appreciates the cosmic tapestry of individuality.

Embark on Your Cosmic Odyssey:

• The journey to understanding your birthday profile is an ongoing adventure. Embrace the mysteries, celebrate your uniqueness, and let the cosmic energies guide you toward a richer, more fulfilling life.

Uncover the cosmic wonders that make you who you are. Your birthday profile is not just a set of numbers and positions; it's a cosmic story waiting to be explored. Happy discovering! ◇◇

Certainly! Here are some tools and quizzes to help readers understand their personality traits based on their birthday profiles in 'The Secret Language of Birthdays April Profiles':

1. **Astrology Birth Chart:**

• **Tool:** Use online astrology websites to generate your full birth chart.

• **How to Use:** Input your birth date, time, and place to get a detailed map of the positions of celestial bodies at your birth. Explore your sun sign, moon sign, rising sign, and more.

2. **Numerology Calculator:**

• **Tool:** Numerology calculators available online.

• **How to Use:** Enter your birthdate to find your life path number, expression number, and other significant numerological aspects. These numbers offer insights into your personality and life journey.

3. **Zodiac Compatibility Quizzes:**

• **Quiz:** Take zodiac compatibility quizzes on astrology websites.

• **How to Use:** Answer questions about your and your partner's zodiac signs to get insights into your compatibility. These quizzes often highlight strengths and potential challenges in relationships.

4. Myers-Briggs Type Indicator (MBTI) Test:

• **Tool:** Online MBTI tests available on various platforms.

• **How to Use:** Take the test to determine your personality type based on preferences in four dichotomies: Extraversion/Introversion, Sensing/Intuition, Thinking/Feeling, and Judging/Perceiving.

5. Enneagram Personality Test:

• **Tool:** Enneagram tests available online.

• **How to Use:** Discover your Enneagram type, a system that categorizes individuals into nine distinct personality types. Each type has its characteristics, motivations, and growth paths.

6. StrengthsFinder Assessment:

• **Tool:** StrengthsFinder assessment available on its official website.

• **How to Use:** Take the assessment to uncover your top strengths out of 34 possible themes. Understand how these strengths shape your approach to work, relationships, and personal development.

7. DISC Personality Test:

- **Tool:** DISC assessments available online.

- **How to Use:** Complete the test to identify your Dominance, Influence, Steadiness, and Conscientiousness traits. Gain insights into your communication style and behavior in various situations.

8. Big Five Personality Test:

- **Tool:** Online platforms offering the Big Five Personality Test.

- **How to Use:** Take the test to assess your openness, conscientiousness, extraversion, agreeableness, and neuroticism. Understand how these factors contribute to your overall personality.

9. Color Personality Quiz:

- **Quiz:** Various color personality quizzes online.

- **How to Use:** Answer questions related to color preferences to uncover aspects of your personality. Different colors are associated with specific traits and characteristics.

These assessments provide general insights and should be taken with a sense of self-reflection and openness to personal growth. Happy exploring!

Emphasize the uniqueness of each individual's birthday influence.

Celebrate the extraordinary tapestry of your individuality, woven by the cosmic threads of your birthday influence in 'The Secret Language of Birthdays April Profiles.' Your birthdate is more than just a number; it's a cosmic signature that paints a unique portrait of who you are. Here's why the uniqueness of your birthday influence is a cause for celebration:

1. **Cosmic Symphony of Elements:**

- Your birthdate is a harmonious blend of astrological elements—Fire, Earth, Air, and Water. Whether you resonate with the fiery passion, the grounded stability, the intellectual air, or the emotional depth of water, your cosmic composition is uniquely yours.

2. **Starry Constellations of Traits:**

- The alignment of planets and stars at the time of your birth shapes your sun sign, moon sign, and rising sign. These celestial constellations bestow upon you a set of traits and qualities that paint a vivid picture of your personality, emphasizing your strengths and potential challenges.

3. **Numerological Symphony:**

- Your birthdate holds the magic of numerology, where each number carries its unique vibration. Your life path number, expression number, and other numerological aspects contribute to the melody of your life, guiding you on your journey of self-discovery.

4. **Individual Zodiac Dance:**

- While zodiac signs share common traits, your individual birthdate refines these characteristics into a personalized dance. Your sun sign, moon sign, and other astrological placements create a choreography of energies that makes you stand out in the cosmic ballroom.

5. Mystical Birth Chart:

• Your astrological birth chart is like a mystical map, outlining the positions of celestial bodies at the moment you entered the world. This unique snapshot of the heavens captures the essence of your cosmic blueprint, influencing your path, purpose, and potential.

6. Diverse Celestial Influences:

• Every planet, from the fiery Mars to the mysterious Neptune, leaves its imprint on your personality. The diverse celestial influences converge to create a nuanced portrait, showcasing the multifaceted nature of your being.

7. Personalized Compatibility Constellation:

• Your compatibility with others is a cosmic dance of elements and energies. Understanding the uniqueness of your birthday influence enhances your connections, allowing you to appreciate the diverse constellations of personalities around you.

8. Dynamic Evolutionary Journey:

• Your birthday influence is not static; it's a dynamic force guiding your evolutionary journey. As you grow, learn, and adapt, the cosmic energies continue to shape and mold your personality, creating a narrative that is uniquely yours.

Embrace the uniqueness of your birthday influence with open arms. Celebrate the cosmic masterpiece that is you, with all your strengths, quirks, and potential waiting to unfold. In 'The Secret

Language of Birthdays April Profiles,' let the exploration of your individual cosmic fingerprint be a joyful and empowering experience.

The Essence of April Birthdays

April birthdays carry a vibrant essence, infused with the freshness of spring and the energy of renewal. Here's a glimpse into the unique qualities that define individuals born in April:

1. **Aries Energy (March 21 - April 19):**

- April kicks off with the dynamic and passionate Aries season. Aries, the first sign of the zodiac, brings a burst of energy, enthusiasm, and a pioneering spirit. April-born individuals often embody the bold and assertive traits associated with this fire sign.

2. **Springtime Vibrancy:**

- April is synonymous with the arrival of spring, marking a period of rebirth and growth. Individuals born during this month often exhibit a lively and optimistic outlook, mirroring the blossoming flowers and the awakening of nature.

3. **Dynamic and Adventurous Spirit:**

- The influence of Aries contributes to an adventurous and courageous demeanor. April-born individuals are not afraid to take risks, explore new territories, and embrace challenges with a spirited approach to life.

4. Natural Leaders:

• Aries, being a cardinal sign, instills natural leadership qualities in those born in April. They possess an innate ability to take charge, initiate projects, and inspire others with their charisma and determination.

5. Creative Expression:

• The artistic influences of Aries, combined with the artistic aura of spring, foster creativity in April-born individuals. Whether in the arts, business, or everyday pursuits, they often express themselves with a unique and imaginative flair.

6. Independent Thinkers:

• April birthdays often exhibit a sense of independence and a desire to carve their own path. The Aries influence encourages a self-reliant and pioneering mindset, making them natural trailblazers in various aspects of life.

7. Energetic and Spontaneous Lifestyle:

• The lively energy of April is reflected in the spontaneous and energetic lifestyle of those born during this month. They thrive on excitement, seek new experiences, and infuse a sense of liveliness into their surroundings.

8. Passionate Pursuits:

• Passion runs deep in the hearts of April-born individuals. Whether pursuing personal relationships, career goals, or hobbies, they approach life with a fervor that is both inspiring and contagious.

9. Balancing Determination and Compassion:

• April birthdays often strike a balance between the determined, assertive nature of Aries and a compassionate, caring side. This blend of qualities allows them to navigate relationships with both strength and empathy.

10. Symbolism of April's Birthstones:

• The birthstones for April, diamonds and clear quartz, symbolize clarity, strength, and invincibility. These stones reflect the resilience and enduring qualities often associated with those born in April.

In 'The Secret Language of Birthdays April Profiles,' the essence of April birthdays is a celebration of vitality, creativity, and the unwavering spirit of those who enter the world during this vibrant month.

Personality Traits: A Deep Dive for April

Delve into the intricacies of the personality traits that shape individuals born in April. While each person is unique, there are common characteristics associated with April birthdays, influenced by the dynamic interplay of astrological and seasonal energies:

1. **Aries' Fiery Spirit:**

 • **Assertiveness:** A dominant trait stems from the Aries zodiac influence, emphasizing a strong and assertive demeanor. April-born individuals often exhibit a go-getter attitude, fearlessly pursuing their goals.

2. **Natural Leadership:**

 • **Leadership Qualities:** Infused with the leadership prowess of Aries, those born in April tend to be natural leaders. Their ability to take charge, make decisions, and inspire others is a key aspect of their personality.

3. **Energetic and Dynamic:**

 • **High Energy Levels:** April individuals are known for their dynamic and vibrant energy. They approach life with enthusiasm, engaging in activities with a zest that energizes both themselves and those around them.

4. Courageous Trailblazers:

- **Fearless Explorers:** The adventurous spirit of Aries manifests in April-born individuals as a fearlessness to explore uncharted territories. They embrace challenges head-on, seeing them as opportunities for growth.

5. Independence and Initiative:

- **Independent Thinkers:** Independence is a hallmark trait. April-born individuals have a strong sense of self, often initiating projects and ventures independently, showcasing their initiative and resourcefulness.

6. Optimistic Outlook:

- **Positive Mindset:** Connected to the arrival of spring, April birthdays often exude optimism. They possess an innate ability to see the brighter side of situations, maintaining a positive outlook even in challenging times.

7. Creative Expression:

- **Artistic Flair:** Fueled by the creative energy of Aries and the blossoming surroundings of spring, April-born individuals often have a natural artistic flair. Whether in the arts, innovation, or problem-solving, creativity is a defining trait.

8. Impulsive yet Spontaneous:

- **Spontaneity:** A touch of impulsiveness adds a spontaneous element to their personalities. April-born individuals are inclined to seize the moment, embracing the excitement of the unknown.

9. Compassion in Relationships:

• **Empathy and Compassion:** Balancing the assertiveness of Aries, individuals born in April display a compassionate side. In relationships, they can be understanding and supportive, fostering deep connections with others.

10. Adaptable Nature:

• **Versatility:** April birthdays often exhibit a versatile nature, adapting to different situations with ease. This adaptability allows them to navigate a variety of circumstances, making them well-rounded individuals.

11. Determined and Resilient:

• **Determination:** Rooted in the Aries spirit, April-born individuals demonstrate determination and resilience. When faced with challenges, they display a tenacity to overcome obstacles and emerge stronger.

12. Balancing Strength and Sensitivity:

• **Harmony in Contrasts:** April birthdays often find a delicate balance between strength and sensitivity. While assertive, they can also be attuned to the emotions of others, creating a harmonious blend of qualities.

In 'The Secret Language of Birthdays April Profiles,' the deep dive into April personality traits reveals a rich tapestry of qualities influenced by Aries' fire and the blossoming energies of spring.

The Zodiac Influence

The zodiac exerts a profound influence on individuals, shaping their personalities based on the positions of celestial bodies at the time of their birth. Here's a brief exploration of the zodiac's impact:

1. **Aries (March 21 - April 19):**

   • Governed by Mars, Aries individuals embody dynamic energy, assertiveness, and a pioneering spirit. They are natural leaders with a zest for adventure.

2. **Taurus (April 20 - May 20):**

   • Ruled by Venus, Taurus individuals are grounded, practical, and value stability. They exhibit determination, reliability, and an appreciation for the finer things in life.

3. **Gemini (May 21 - June 20):**

   • Mercury governs Gemini, fostering curiosity, versatility, and excellent communication skills. Geminis are social, adaptable, and thrive in diverse situations.

4. **Cancer (June 21 - July 22):**

• The Moon influences Cancer, instilling emotional depth, intuition, and strong familial bonds. Cancer individuals are nurturing, empathetic, and value security.

5. Leo (July 23 - August 22):

• Ruled by the Sun, Leos exude confidence, charisma, and a flair for the dramatic. They are natural leaders with a generous and warm-hearted nature.

6. Virgo (August 23 - September 22):

• Governed by Mercury, Virgos are analytical, detail-oriented, and possess a strong sense of duty. They excel in practical tasks and strive for perfection.

7. Libra (September 23 - October 22):

• Venus influences Libra, fostering a love for harmony, diplomacy, and aesthetic pursuits. Libras are social, fair-minded, and seek balance in relationships.

8. Scorpio (October 23 - November 21):

• Ruled by Pluto, Scorpios embody intensity, passion, and a deep sense of mystery. They are determined, resourceful, and value authenticity.

9. Sagittarius (November 22 - December 21):

• Governed by Jupiter, Sagittarians are adventurous, optimistic, and love intellectual pursuits. They seek freedom, enjoy exploration, and have a philosophical outlook.

10. Capricorn (December 22 - January 19):

- Saturn influences Capricorn, imparting discipline, ambition, and a strong sense of responsibility. Capricorns are practical, goal-oriented, and value hard work.

11. Aquarius (January 20 - February 18):

- Ruled by Uranus, Aquarians are known for their originality, humanitarian values, and open-mindedness. They are visionaries who embrace innovation.

12. Pisces (February 19 - March 20):

- Governed by Neptune, Pisceans are empathetic, artistic, and have a deep connection to the mystical. They are intuitive, compassionate, and often creative individuals.

The zodiac, with its twelve distinct signs, provides a framework for understanding and appreciating the diverse traits and tendencies that shape individuals based on their birth dates. Each sign contributes unique qualities, fostering a rich tapestry of personalities across the zodiac spectrum.

5. Celebrating April: Traditions and Customs

Celebrating April: Traditions and Customs

April brings forth a tapestry of traditions and customs, marking the transition into spring and celebrating various cultural and historical events. Here's a glimpse into the festivities associated with April:

1. **April Fools' Day (April 1st):**

  • April kicks off with humor as people engage in playful pranks and jokes on April Fools' Day. The day is dedicated to light-hearted mischief, bringing laughter and surprise.

2. **Easter Celebrations (Date Varies):**

  • Easter, a significant Christian holiday, often falls in April. Traditions include Easter egg hunts, feasts, and religious services commemorating the resurrection of Jesus Christ.

3. **National Poetry Month:**

  • April is designated as National Poetry Month, celebrating the art of poetry. It encourages the reading and writing of poems, with events and activities held worldwide to honor poets and their contributions.

4. Earth Day (April 22nd):

• Earth Day focuses on environmental awareness and conservation efforts. Activities include tree planting, clean-up initiatives, and educational events to promote sustainable practices.

5. International Dance Day (April 29th):

• A day dedicated to the art of dance, International Dance Day celebrates the universal language of movement. Events, performances, and dance classes take place globally to honor this expressive form.

6. Cherry Blossom Festivals:

• In various parts of the world, especially in Japan and the United States, April heralds cherry blossom festivals. These events showcase the beauty of cherry blossoms, symbolizing renewal and the fleeting nature of life.

7. National Arbor Day (Last Friday in April):

• Arbor Day encourages tree planting and environmental stewardship. Communities participate in tree-planting activities, fostering a sense of responsibility towards nature.

8. Passover (Date Varies):

• For the Jewish community, April may coincide with Passover, a significant festival commemorating the liberation of the Israelites from slavery in ancient Egypt. Traditions include a special meal, the Seder.

9. Administrative Professionals' Day (Date Varies):

- Celebrated in April, this day honors the contributions of administrative professionals in the workplace. Colleagues express appreciation through gestures and gifts.

10. World Book Day (April 23rd):

- World Book Day celebrates the joy of reading and promotes literacy. Activities include book fairs, storytelling sessions, and initiatives to share the love of literature.

April's diverse traditions encompass laughter, reflection, environmental consciousness, and cultural celebrations. Whether through playful pranks or solemn religious observances, the customs associated with April reflect a rich tapestry of global heritage.

6. April Birthstones and Their Significance

April Birthstones and Their Significance

April, a month of burgeoning spring, is associated with two enchanting birthstones—diamond and clear quartz. These precious gems hold unique significance and symbolism for individuals born in this vibrant month:

1. **Diamond:**

- **Significance:** Diamonds symbolize enduring love, strength, and purity. Their exceptional hardness reflects the resilience and everlasting nature of relationships. Diamonds are often used in engagement rings, symbolizing eternal commitment.

- **Properties:** Known for their brilliance and clarity, diamonds come in various cuts and colors. The most prized diamonds are colorless and exhibit a dazzling sparkle.

2. **Clear Quartz:**

- **Significance:** Clear quartz is renowned for its healing properties and spiritual significance. It is believed to amplify energy, promote clarity of thought, and enhance spiritual awareness. Clear quartz is associated with balance and harmony.

• **Properties:** As a colorless and transparent gemstone, clear quartz is versatile and often used in jewelry. It is also valued in alternative therapies and spiritual practices for its purported metaphysical qualities.

These April birthstones, with their distinct qualities, offer individuals not only aesthetic beauty but also deeper connections to love, resilience, spirituality, and clarity of thought. Whether adorned as jewelry or used for metaphysical purposes, these gems enhance the significance of one's birth month.

7. Relationships and Compatibility for people born in april 2000 words

Relationships and Compatibility for April Birthdays

Individuals born in April carry the dynamic energy of Aries or the grounded stability of Taurus, depending on their specific birthdate. Understanding the astrological influences can provide insights into relationships and compatibility.

Aries (March 21 - April 19):
Traits:

1. **Passionate and Dynamic:** Aries individuals are known for their fiery passion and dynamic nature. They bring enthusiasm and energy into relationships.
2. **Assertive Leadership:** Natural leaders, Aries can take charge and make decisions. Their assertiveness can be attractive, but it requires a partner who appreciates their independence.
3. **Adventurous Spirit:** Aries loves excitement and adventure, making them ideal companions for spontaneous and thrilling experiences.

Compatibility:
1. Leo (July 23 - August 22):

• Both Aries and Leo share a passion for life, love challenges, and have a dynamic approach. Their adventurous spirits align well, creating a vibrant and exciting partnership.

2. **Sagittarius (November 22 - December 21):**

• The adventurous nature of Aries harmonizes with Sagittarius' love for exploration. Both signs seek freedom and intellectual pursuits, fostering a dynamic and stimulating relationship.

3. **Gemini (May 21 - June 20):**

• Gemini's versatility complements Aries' energy. The duo can engage in lively conversations and feed each other's need for mental stimulation, creating a dynamic and communicative bond.

Taurus (April 20 - May 20):
Traits:

1. **Stable and Grounded:** Taurus individuals bring stability and a grounded nature to relationships. They value security and often seek long-term commitments.
2. **Patient and Reliable:** Taurus partners are patient and reliable, providing a steady presence in the lives of their loved ones. Trust and dependability are crucial to them.
3. **Appreciation for Comfort:** Taurus appreciates the finer things in life and enjoys creating a comfortable and aesthetically pleasing environment.

Compatibility:
1. **Virgo (August 23 - September 22):**

• Both Taurus and Virgo value stability and share a practical approach to life. Their attention to detail and reliability create a harmonious and enduring connection.

2. Capricorn (December 22 - January 19):

• Taurus and Capricorn appreciate each other's commitment to long-term goals. Their shared values of hard work and stability form the foundation for a strong and enduring relationship.

3. Cancer (June 21 - July 22):

• Cancer's nurturing nature complements Taurus' need for security. The emotional connection between these signs fosters a supportive and loving partnership.

Understanding astrological traits provides a glimpse into potential compatibility, but individual personalities play a crucial role. Communication, mutual respect, and shared values remain key elements for any successful relationship, allowing individuals born in April to create lasting and fulfilling connections.

8. Famous April Birthdays in Pop Cultur

Famous April Birthdays in Pop Culture

April welcomes the birth of numerous influential figures in pop culture, spanning various fields. Here's a glimpse into some iconic personalities born in April:

1. **Robert Downey Jr. (April 4, 1965):**

   • Known for portraying Iron Man in the Marvel Cinematic Universe, Downey Jr. has left an indelible mark on the film industry, combining charisma with versatile acting.

2. **Maya Angelou (April 4, 1928):**

   • A celebrated poet, author, and civil rights activist, Angelou's impactful literary works, including "I Know Why the Caged Bird Sings," continue to resonate globally.

3. **Leonardo da Vinci (April 15, 1452):**

   • The epitome of a Renaissance polymath, da Vinci's contributions as a painter, sculptor, inventor, and scientist remain unparalleled, influencing art and science for centuries.

4. **Emma Watson (April 15, 1990):**

• Best known as Hermione Granger in the Harry Potter film series, Watson has evolved into a prominent actress, UN Women Goodwill Ambassador, and advocate for women's rights.

5. Charlie Chaplin (April 16, 1889):

• A pioneer in silent film, Chaplin's comedic genius and iconic character "The Tramp" have left an enduring legacy in the history of cinema.

6. Queen Elizabeth II (April 21, 1926):

• The longest-reigning monarch in British history, Queen Elizabeth II has witnessed significant historical events during her reign, making her an iconic figure globally.

7. Shakespeare's Birthday (April 23, 1564):

• While the exact date remains uncertain, April 23 is widely celebrated as William Shakespeare's birthday. His plays and sonnets have profoundly influenced literature and drama.

8. Barbra Streisand (April 24, 1942):

• A powerhouse in the entertainment industry, Streisand is a singer, actress, and filmmaker, earning numerous accolades, including multiple Grammy and Academy Awards.

9. Shirley Temple (April 23, 1928):

• A beloved child actress, Temple's charm and talent captivated audiences during the 1930s. She remains an enduring symbol of Hollywood's Golden Age.

10. **Al Pacino (April 25, 1940):**

• An iconic actor with a prolific career, Pacino's roles in films like "The Godfather" and "Scarface" have solidified his status as one of the greatest actors of his generation.

These famous April birthdays have left an indelible impact on the realms of entertainment, literature, art, and politics, shaping the cultural landscape for generations.

9. Career Paths Aligned with April Traits

Career Paths Aligned with April Traits

Individuals born in April, influenced by the dynamic energy of Aries or the grounded stability of Taurus, possess unique traits that can flourish in specific career paths. Here are potential career options that align with April traits:

Aries (March 21 - April 19):

1. Entrepreneurship:

• Aries individuals thrive in dynamic, fast-paced environments. Their assertiveness and natural leadership make them well-suited for entrepreneurial ventures where they can take charge and drive innovation.

2. Sales and Marketing:

• The persuasive and energetic nature of Aries aligns with roles in sales and marketing. Their ability to navigate challenges and enthusiasm for achieving goals can lead to success in these fields.

3. Emergency Services:

• Aries' fearless and quick decision-making skills make them apt for careers in emergency services such as firefighting, paramedics, or law enforcement, where rapid responses are crucial.

4. Sports and Athletics:

• The competitive spirit of Aries lends itself well to careers in sports and athletics. Whether as athletes, coaches, or sports management professionals, Aries individuals thrive in challenging and competitive environments.

Taurus (April 20 - May 20):
1. Finance and Banking:

• Taurus individuals' stability and practicality make them well-suited for roles in finance and banking. Their patient and reliable nature is valuable in managing financial matters.

2. Real Estate:

• The appreciation for comfort and aesthetics in Taurus aligns with careers in real estate. Taurus individuals can excel in property management, real estate development, or interior design.

3. Culinary Arts:

• Taurus individuals often have a keen appreciation for the finer things in life, making them excellent candidates for careers in the culinary arts. From chefs to restaurateurs, their love for creating enjoyable experiences shines.

4. Environmental Conservation:

• Taurus' connection to nature and appreciation for stability can lead to fulfilling careers in environmental conservation. Roles in sustainable practices, landscaping, or wildlife preservation align with their values.

Understanding these astrological traits can provide guidance for individuals born in April as they explore potential career paths. However, personal interests, skills, and passions should always play a crucial role in shaping one's professional journey.

10. Health and Wellness Insights for people born in april

Health and Wellness Insights for April Birthdays

Individuals born in April, influenced by the energetic Aries or the grounded Taurus, possess unique characteristics that can guide their approach to health and wellness. Here are insights tailored to April birthdays:

Aries (March 21 - April 19):

1. **Active Lifestyle:**

• Aries individuals thrive on activity and movement. Engage in dynamic exercises that align with your energetic nature. Sports, high-intensity workouts, and outdoor activities can be particularly enjoyable.

2. **Mind-Body Connection:**

• Aries' mental energy can sometimes lead to stress. Incorporate mindfulness practices such as meditation and yoga to balance your active mind with a sense of calm and focus.

3. **Consistent Exercise Routine:**

• Aries individuals benefit from consistent exercise routines. Establish a regular schedule for workouts to maintain physical health and channel your abundant energy positively.

4. Balanced Nutrition:

• Aries individuals may overlook nutritional aspects in their busy lives. Focus on a balanced diet rich in protein, complex carbohydrates, and fresh fruits and vegetables to sustain your energy levels.

Taurus (April 20 - May 20):
1. Stress Management:

• Taurus individuals may carry stress in their determined pursuit of goals. Incorporate stress-management techniques such as deep breathing, meditation, or leisurely activities to maintain emotional well-being.

2. Regular Exercise in Nature:

• Taurus individuals have a strong connection to nature. Opt for outdoor exercises like walking, hiking, or gardening to align with your appreciation for the natural world.

3. Mindful Eating:

• Taurus' love for comfort and aesthetics extends to food. Practice mindful eating, savoring each bite and paying attention to portion sizes, to ensure a healthy relationship with food.

4. Establishing Routine:

- Taurus benefits from a consistent routine. Create a balanced daily schedule that includes regular meals, sufficient sleep, and dedicated time for self-care to support overall wellness.

Remember, while astrological insights can provide general guidance, individual health needs vary. Consulting with healthcare professionals and incorporating personalized wellness practices based on your unique circumstances is crucial for maintaining optimal health.

Navigating Challenges: April Birthdays

Individuals born in April, under the influence of Aries or Taurus, may face distinct challenges. Understanding these challenges and adopting proactive approaches can contribute to personal growth and resilience.

Aries (March 21 - April 19):
1. **Impulsiveness:**

• Challenge: Aries individuals may struggle with impulsive decision-making.

• Approach: Practice mindfulness and take a moment to reflect before making significant choices. Seeking advice from others can provide valuable perspectives.

2. **Patience in Relationships:**

• Challenge: Aries' energetic nature may lead to impatience in relationships.

• Approach: Cultivate patience by actively listening and considering the perspectives of others. Practice empathy to strengthen interpersonal connections.

3. **Balancing Energy Levels:**

• Challenge: Maintaining consistent energy levels can be challenging for Aries.

• Approach: Establish a balanced routine that includes adequate rest and regular, sustainable physical activities. Avoid burnout by recognizing the importance of pacing.

Taurus (April 20 - May 20):

1. **Resistance to Change:**

• Challenge: Taurus individuals may resist change, hindering adaptability.

• Approach: Embrace change gradually, focusing on its potential positive outcomes. Develop a mindset that views change as an opportunity for growth.

2. **Stubbornness:**

• Challenge: Taurus' determination can sometimes manifest as stubbornness.

• Approach: Practice open-mindedness and flexibility. Recognize situations where compromise is beneficial, fostering better collaboration with others.

3. **Managing Stress:**

• Challenge: Taurus individuals may accumulate stress due to a strong drive for success.

• Approach: Incorporate stress-management techniques such as mindfulness, relaxation exercises, and regular breaks. Recognize when it's essential to step back and prioritize self-care.

Navigating challenges is a universal aspect of personal development. April birthdays can leverage their unique traits to overcome obstacles and cultivate resilience. Seeking support from friends, family, or professional resources can enhance the journey of self-improvement.

April's Impact on Creativity

April, with its unique astrological influences from Aries and Taurus, can significantly impact creativity. Understanding these influences provides insights into how individuals born in April can harness their creative potential.

Aries (March 21 - April 19):

1. Energetic Sparks:

- Aries individuals are fueled by dynamic energy, sparking creativity. Their enthusiasm and bold approach to life often translate into innovative ideas and ventures.

2. Fearless Exploration:

- The fearless nature of Aries encourages creative exploration. They are more likely to embrace new and unconventional concepts, pushing the boundaries of traditional thinking.

3. Quick Inspirations:

- Aries' quick decision-making extends to creative pursuits. They are adept at swiftly turning inspirations into tangible projects, making them dynamic creators in various fields.

4. Leadership in Creative Projects:

• Aries' natural leadership qualities position them as catalysts in creative endeavors. They can take charge and inspire others, steering collaborative projects with confidence.

Taurus (April 20 - May 20):
1. Stability and Consistency:

• Taurus individuals bring stability and consistency to their creative process. Their methodical approach ensures that creative projects are well-grounded and enduring.

2. Appreciation for Aesthetics:

• Taurus' love for comfort and aesthetics reflects in their creative endeavors. They often infuse beauty and sensory richness into their work, whether it be art, design, or other creative expressions.

3. Patient Craftsmanship:

• Taurus individuals exhibit patience in crafting their creative projects. This patience results in meticulous attention to detail, producing high-quality and aesthetically pleasing outcomes.

4. Sensual Inspiration:

• Taurus draws inspiration from the senses, incorporating sensory experiences into their creative pursuits. Music, art, and other sensory stimuli play a crucial role in fueling their imaginative process.

Understanding the astrological traits of Aries and Taurus can guide individuals in optimizing their creative potential. Whether it's the dynamic and energetic approach of Aries or the grounded and aesthetic sensibilities of Taurus, April's impact on creativity is diverse and enriching.

Parenting a child born in April

Parenting a child born in April, influenced by the dynamic energy of Aries or the grounded stability of Taurus, comes with its unique joys and challenges. Understanding the astrological traits associated with April births can guide parents in fostering a supportive and nurturing environment for their child.

Aries (March 21 - April 19):

1. Encourage Independence:

- Aries children are known for their independent nature. Encourage and support their autonomy, allowing them to make decisions and explore their interests.

2. Channel Energy Positively:

- Aries is full of energy and enthusiasm. Provide outlets for physical activities and creative pursuits to channel their abundant energy in positive ways.

3. Teach Patience and Teamwork:

- Aries children may benefit from learning patience and teamwork. Engage them in activities that involve cooperation and emphasize the value of working with others.

4. Celebrate Achievements:

• Aries children thrive on recognition. Celebrate their achievements, no matter how small, to boost their confidence and foster a positive self-image.

Taurus (April 20 - May 20):
1. Create a Stable Routine:

• Taurus children appreciate stability. Establish a consistent daily routine that provides a sense of security and helps them thrive.

2. Encourage Creativity:

• Taurus children often have a creative flair. Support and encourage their artistic expressions, whether through art, music, or imaginative play.

3. Teach Financial Responsibility:

• Taurus values financial stability. Introduce basic financial concepts and encourage responsible money habits to instill a sense of financial awareness.

4. Promote Healthy Eating Habits:

• Taurus is associated with an appreciation for good food. Use this as an opportunity to instill healthy eating habits, introducing a variety of nutritious foods into their diet.

Remember that while astrological traits provide a broad framework, each child is unique. Pay attention to their individual needs, preferences, and developmental milestones. Effective parenting involves a balance of understanding astrological influences and responding to the unique personality of your April-born child.

Social Connections: April's Social Butterflies

Individuals born in April, influenced by the dynamic energy of Aries or the grounded stability of Taurus, tend to be social butterflies with distinctive qualities that contribute to vibrant connections. Understanding these traits can enhance social interactions and relationships.

Aries (March 21 - April 19):

1. Enthusiastic Communicators:

• Aries individuals are known for their enthusiastic and direct communication style. They express themselves with energy, making interactions lively and engaging.

2. Initiators of Social Activities:

• Aries, being natural leaders, often take the lead in organizing social gatherings. Their dynamic nature makes them adept at planning and executing events that bring people together.

3. Loyalty in Friendships:

- Aries values loyalty in friendships. Once they form a connection, they are committed and supportive, fostering strong and enduring bonds with those they care about.

4. Adventurous Companions:

- Aries individuals thrive on excitement and adventure. They make fantastic companions for spontaneous activities, exploring new places, and embracing the thrill of the moment.

Taurus (April 20 - May 20):
1. Steadfast and Reliable Friends:

- Taurus individuals are reliable and steadfast in their friendships. They build trust over time, becoming dependable and supportive friends who value long-lasting connections.

2. Social Gatherings with Comfort:

- Taurus enjoys socializing in comfortable settings. Whether it's a cozy dinner or a relaxed gathering, they create environments where people feel at ease and can connect effortlessly.

3. Appreciation for Quality Time:

- Taurus values quality time spent with friends. They cherish meaningful conversations and shared experiences, emphasizing the depth and sincerity of their social connections.

4. Generosity in Relationships:

- Taurus individuals often express their social warmth through gestures of generosity. Whether it's hosting gatherings or offering support, their generosity strengthens the bonds they form.

Understanding the social tendencies of April-born individuals can enhance the richness of friendships and social connections. Whether it's the dynamic and direct approach of Aries or the steadfast and comforting presence of Taurus, April's social butterflies contribute vibrancy to the tapestry of relationships.

Wisdom and Life Lessons from April Birthdays

Individuals born in April, under the influence of Aries or Taurus, carry unique qualities that contribute to valuable life lessons and wisdom. These insights can guide their personal growth and enhance their journey through life.

Aries (March 21 - April 19):

1. **Embrace Fearlessness:**

- Aries individuals teach us the power of fearlessness. Embracing challenges with courage and a positive mindset allows for personal growth and the conquering of obstacles.

2. **Live in the Present:**

- Aries' dynamic nature emphasizes living in the present moment. The ability to seize opportunities and appreciate the now contributes to a fulfilling and enriching life.

3. **Leadership and Initiative:**

- Aries' natural leadership qualities teach the importance of taking initiative. Leading with confidence and decisiveness can open doors to success and inspire others.

4. Learn from Setbacks:

- Aries individuals understand the value of learning from setbacks. Instead of being discouraged, use challenges as opportunities for growth and development.

Taurus (April 20 - May 20):
1. Appreciate Stability:

- Taurus teaches us the significance of stability. Embracing a stable foundation in various aspects of life, including relationships and career, provides a sense of security.

2. Value Patience:

- Taurus individuals emphasize the virtue of patience. Understanding that some things take time allows for the development of resilience and a more balanced perspective.

3. Celebrate Sensory Experiences:

- Taurus' appreciation for the senses encourages us to celebrate sensory experiences. Taking the time to indulge in the pleasures of taste, touch, and sight enhances life's richness.

4. Build Lasting Relationships:

- Taurus values lasting and meaningful relationships. Investing time and effort into building strong connections fosters a sense of community and support.

Wisdom from April birthdays is diverse, encompassing fearlessness, living in the present, leadership, stability, patience, sensory appreciation, and building lasting relationships. Incorporating these lessons into life can contribute to a well-rounded and fulfilling journey.

We extend our sincere thanks to you, dear readers, for embarking on this astrological journey with us. Your curiosity, engagement, and trust have made this exploration of the Zodiac sign Cancer all the more fulfilling.

In these pages, we have delved into the essence of the Cancer sign, unveiling its secrets, traits, and the horoscope for 2024. We've ventured through the depths of emotion, explored the intricacies of relationships, and discovered the likes and dislikes of a Cancer individual. All of this would not have been possible without your interest and presence.

Your quest for knowledge and self-discovery is what fuels our passion for astrology, and we are grateful to have been your guides in this cosmic voyage. We hope that the insights and wisdom shared in these pages serve as a guiding light in your life.

We invite you to explore our other books, each dedicated to a unique Zodiac sign and various aspects of astrology. Whether you seek to deepen your understanding of the stars or uncover the mysteries of other signs, you'll find a wealth of knowledge waiting for you.

Should you have any questions, insights, or simply wish to connect with us, please don't hesitate to reach out.

You can contact us via WhatsApp at +1 829-205-5456 or email us at danielsanjurjo47@gmail.com.

May the stars continue to shine brightly on your path, and may your journey through the Zodiac signs be filled with enlightenment, growth, and harmony. Sincerely Daniel Sanjurjo

About the Author

Daniel Sanjurjo is a passionate author who delves into the realms of astrology and self-help. With a gift for exploring the celestial and the human psyche, Daniel's books are celestial journeys of self-discovery and personal growth. Join the cosmic odyssey with this insightful writer.

Don't miss out!

Visit the website below and you can sign up to receive emails whenever Daniel Sanjurjo publishes a new book. There's no charge and no obligation.

https://books2read.com/r/B-A-WQHBB-RRAUC

BOOKS 2 READ

Connecting independent readers to independent writers.

Did you love *The Secret Language of Birthdays April Profiles*? Then you should read *Dreams Interpretation Guide*[1] by Daniel Sanjurjo!

[2]

◇ Unlock the Secrets of Dreams with "Dreamscape Chronicles: A Journey into the World of Dreams"

◇ Are you ready to embark on a profound dream interpretation journey that will unveil the hidden meanings of your dreams, offering insights into your inner self, personal growth, and self-discovery? "Dreamscape Chronicles" is your definitive guide to navigating the enigmatic landscapes of the subconscious mind.

◇ Explore the Depths of Dream Analysis: Delve into the intricate world of dream interpretation, where the symbols and stories of the night come alive. From common dreams to the mysteries of the mind,

---

1. https://books2read.com/u/38Ykxd

2. https://books2read.com/u/38Ykxd

this book unravels the symbolism and significance of your dreamscapes.

◇ Illuminate Your Path: Discover how dreams can inspire your creativity, provide therapeutic insights, and awaken your inner desires. This book serves as your compass, guiding you through the rich tapestry of dreams and helping you harness their potential.

◇ Key Topics Explored: Uncover the significance of dream symbolism, the role of common dream themes, and the influence of pioneers like Sigmund Freud in understanding the profound landscapes of the dreamer's mind.

Are you ready to embark on a journey through the dreamer's world? "Dreamscape Chronicles" is your passport to the boundless landscapes of your own mind. Explore, interpret, and awaken to the possibilities hidden within your dreams.

Unlock the mysteries of your dreams and start your journey of self-discovery today!

Also by Daniel Sanjurjo

Birthdays Profiles
The Secret Language of Birthdays Profiles - January Personality
Insights.
The Secret Language of Birthdays - February Personality Insights
The Secret Language of Birthdays March Profiles
The Secret Language of Birthdays April Profiles

Zodiaco
Aries 2024 Mes Por Mes
Tauro 2024 Mes Por Mes
Géminis 2024 Mes Por Mes
Cáncer 2024 Mes Por Mes
Leo 2024 Mes Por Mes:
Virgo 2024 Mes Por Mes
Libra 2024 Mes Por Mes
Escorpio 2024 Mes Por Mes
Sagitario 2024 Mes Por Mes
Capricornio 2024 Mes Por Mes
Acuario 2024 Mes Por Mes
Piscis 2024: Un Viaje Celestial
Piscis 2024 Mes Por Mes

Zodiac world
Aries Revealed 2024
Taurus 2024
Leo 2024
Gemini 2024
Cancer horoscope 2024
Virgo 2024
Scorpio 2024
Sagittarius 2024
Capricorn 2024
Aquarius 2024

Standalone
Cosmic Revelations 2024
Dreams Interpretation Guide
Explorando Mis Sueños: Descubre el Mundo Fascinante de tu Mente
Nocturna
Moon And Astrology Planner 2024
Numerology 101 Beginner's Guide to Numerology

www.ingramcontent.com/pod-product-compliance
Lightning Source LLC
Chambersburg PA
CBHW061445150726
47987CB00001B/346